THE
TRANSFORMING
POWER
OF
STORY

WHAT PEOPLE ARE SAYING ABOUT THIS BOOK:

"Eng and Biebel have privileged their readers to hear directly from survivors. The storytellers are ones who painfully looked for and found who they could trust to transform the chaos of the wounded soul to become a dependable guidepost of encouragement and healing. This book includes menus for practical applications, allowing any of us to create help for others from our own lessons of loss."

–Marvin Jewell, MD
Christian Medical and Dental Education Commission

The Transforming Power of Story not only talks about why our stories are so important to share, but it also demonstrates this fact through each story recounted in this book. I know that as an adult missionary kid, until I understood my story and realized that despite all the good of my life, there were cycles of grief and loss I had never dealt with, thus I had no way to address the dark nights of the soul I often felt. Through the exercises at the end of each chapter, this ground-breaking book gives opportunity for each reader to reflect on his or her life story in ways that give the just-read story practical application in the reader's life. A great job. A great read. A potentially life changing book."

–Ruth E. Van Reken, author, *Letters Never Sent* (my story!),
and co-author, *Third Culture Kids: Growing Up Among Worlds*

"Each story is gripping. We have met other couples who face similar transitions. You've given us a new vision of the power of a 'Tell Your Story' forum in the 'community of illnesses' in which we now find ourselves."

-Sharon Ellison and Craig Ellison, PhD, author of:
From Stress to Well-Being

THE TRANSFORMING POWER OF STORY

HOW TELLING YOUR STORY BRINGS HOPE TO OTHERS AND HEALING TO YOURSELF

ELAINE LEONG ENG, MD

AND

DAVID B. BIEBEL, DMIN

Healthy Life Press
Roseland, Florida

THE TRANSFORMING POWER OF STORY
How Telling Your Story Brings Hope
To Others and Healing to Yourself

Copyright © 2010
by Elaine Leong Eng, MD and David B. Biebel, DMin
Note: Copyright originally submitted and registered as "Christian
Womanhood" (Library of Congress May 16, 2002).

Published by:
Healthy Life Press, PO Box 642, Roseland, FL 32957-0642
www.healthylifepress.com

Cover Design by Judy Johnson

Printed in the United States of America

Library of Congress Cataloging-in-Publication Data
Eng, Elaine Leong
The Transforming Power of Story / David B. Biebel

ISBN 978-1-4515-2996-8

1. Christian Living; 2. Self-help; 3. Group Study

Most Healthy Life Press resources are available worldwide through bookstores and online outlets, depending on their format. This book also exists in a downloadable and printable PDF from www.healthylifepress.com. Distribution of printed or eBook formatted copies violate international copyright law, and are strictly forbidden.

Undesignated Scripture references are taken from the New American Standard Bible. Copyright© 1960, 1962, 1963, 1968, 1971, 1972, 1973, 1975, 1977 by the Lockman Foundation. Used by permission. Scripture references marked (KJV) are taken from King James Version. Those marked (NKJV) are from the New King James Version. Those marked (NIV) are from the Holy Bible, New International Version®. Copyright© 1973, 1978, 1984 by the International Bible Society. Used by permission. All rights reserved. Other versions used are noted in the text.

DEDICATION

This book is dedicated to Allison, Brian, Genevieve, Lauren, Merrill, Michael, Rebecca, and Robert and to all the students who faithfully serve God in their studies.

ACKNOWLEDGEMENTS:

Much thanks is due to the following people for their valuable assistance in the writing of this book:

Dr. Al Weir, Dr. Steve Brown, Dr. Barry Wu, Ms. Ingrid Kjeldaas.

We also express our heartfelt gratitude to all who contributed chapters or portions of chapters. Indeed, this book is a labor of love from all of us to anyone who may be helped by it.

Publisher's notes:

Note 1: Regarding the voice of this book. In chapters not attributed to another contributor, when "I" is used, it is the voice of Dr. Eng."

Note 2: A significant portion of the net proceeds from this book will help fund the work of the Christian Medical & Dental Associations' Continuing Medical & Dental Education program, which helps missionary doctors fulfill their Continuing Medical Education requirements, and thus maintain their licensure. Information about the work of the Christian Medical & Dental Associations can be found in the Appendix related to Organizations.

TABLE OF CONTENTS

FOREWORD
by Gloria Halverson, MD

"To be a person is to have a story to tell." —Isak Dinesen

"There is no agony like bearing an untold story inside of you."
—Maya Angelou

It seems appropriate for a book about storytelling to share with you a few brief stories about the author, Dr. Elaine Eng.

My first experience of Elaine Eng was glimpsing her across a well manicured lawn walking with a white cane in one hand and holding the elbow of another woman. They were walking and talking. She was listening to a story. The other woman saw the grounds around them and led the way. Elaine saw behind the story into the heart and soul and led the way from a difficult life situation to a place of greater understanding and peace. This was in Kenya, Africa. The date and place have changed. The woman to whom the elbow belonged has changed. But I've seen Elaine over and over take this walk and listen to another's story and give her gift of insight. She has walked alongside me.

"Their story, yours, and mine – it's what we all carry with us on this trip we take, and we owe it to each other to respect our stories and learn from them." —William Carlos William

I saw Elaine as she stood at the podium in a crowded classroom outside Chiang Mai, Thailand. She was giving a lecture and was using no notes. Medical principles, Scripture verses, and her own story to illustrate flowed smoothly from her. At the conclusion, there was great applause. The question and answer time started. A missionary doctor stood, having already heard lectures from many medical experts throughout the last several days at this conference. "This hour alone," he said, "was worth the cost of the airfare to come here."

9

"The universe is made up of stories, not atoms." –Muriel Rukeyser

We are at the airport in Bangkok. Elaine joins us at the gate for the first leg of our international flight. She has flown to this conference alone. Her courage comes from her reliance on God.

I see Elaine standing at a podium to address an audience of women physicians who have gathered from all over the United States. Not only does she give two keynote addresses, but spends the rest of the conference with women, one on one, listening to their stories, ministering to their needs.

These are just a few glimpses of Elaine Eng, a remarkable woman, physician, Christian, wife and mother, and friend. Through Elaine, I also glimpse God, as Elaine lives such a full life with peace and joy, despite a handicap that could be expected to cause so much more disability.

"If stories come to you, care for them. And learn to give them away where they are needed. Sometimes a person needs a story more than food to stay alive." —Barry Lopez, in *Crow and Weasel*

It was Rwanda 1997. A small group of us from the U.S. were there to minister to women who had been brutalized, but had physically survived the genocide. How do three American women bridge not just a physical but a cultural and experiential ocean and even begin to relate and help? The first day's "teaching" time was short. We basically said, "Tell us your stories," and they then proceeded to teach us. We were bound together through listening, through sharing, through tears, through hugs, through prayers. God was present in a mighty way.

Yes, tell me your story... Dr. Eng's basic lesson of this book – the importance of stories and how to facilitate their telling – is a skill that we can all learn and use to grow, share, relate, heal, and motivate.

"Go out and let stories happen to you, work them, water them with your blood and tears and laughter until they bloom and until you yourself burst into bloom" –Anonymous

PROLOGUE

This book manuscript has a dramatic and puzzling story of its own. I sent the initial chapters to the Library of Congress early this decade for copyright application, but they were trapped in a warehouse due to the "anthrax threat" following September 11, 2001.

After it was unearthed and processed, the registration letter came a full two years later. Much of the work was then completed and sent to the publisher of my other two books, the Haworth Pastoral Press, in 2006. Perturbed by the unusually long response time to my book proposal, which usually had occurred within thirty days, I finally called them after a number of months had gone by and was notified with apologies that my manuscript, along with many others, had been lost in a torrential flood that caused substantial damage to their building in Binghamton, NY.

I sent them another copy at their request. When a rejection letter came from a reviewer different from the familiar, knowledgeable, and enthusiastic hand of Dr. Harold Koenig, the publisher's consultant for the pastoral division, I was stymied. A year later, the reason for this became clear when the Haworth Press sent out an announcement that they were concluding the process of being acquired by another publisher. Consistent with the odd review I received previously, they did not have resources for processing or marketing books on faith.

The pilgrimage of this book manuscript was barred by terrorism in Washington D.C., a natural disaster in upstate New York, and sudden market forces among publishing companies. How can one explain these happenings? I will leave it to the reader to ponder this story.

Meanwhile, a long-time friend, Dr. David Biebel, had founded a new publishing house in 2008, with a mission thoroughly consistent with this book's goals. In the spirit of the God who helps me to persevere, I submitted this book for publication with both trepidation and anticipation of more surprises to come.

–Elaine Leong Eng, MD

TELLING YOUR STORY

During my medical training, I began to lose my vision. In the process, God gave me the grace to learn many lessons through this experience. In print, in counseling, and on the speaker's platform, I have told my story. I have shared the unusual struggles I faced as a wife, mother, OB/Gyn doctor, and finally as a blind psychiatrist. I did this in the hope of helping others.

Ironically, however, despite my background as a psychiatrist, it took me years to realize that sharing my story of coping with blindness helped me as much as it helped others. Telling my story helped me understand its purpose, allowing me to identify with others. It gave me a legacy, and built friendships that I would not have had. Each of these therapeutic benefits has a spiritual implication.

Telling your story will give you the same benefits. Acting as a catalyst to help others share their stories will allow you to help them. My hope and prayer is that this book will accomplish these things in your life.

By talking about my life, I have been able to hear, reframe, and process my own story to understand it and give it meaning. The struggles, catastrophic events, and suffering, as well as the joyful experiences in life, all serve a purpose in the eyes of God and man. The account of Job's life is a perfect illustration. As he told his story to different listeners – his wife, his friends, and the Lord – he undoubtedly learned more about himself and the meaning of his condition.

Theologically, neither Job nor his audiences understood God's purposes in Job's calamities, yet the many opportunities Job had to tell his story enabled him to continually process his perspective and finally accept God's revelation and comfort.

Another healing factor in telling our stories is the power we receive from our audience as we identify with them. When others listen to my story, it gives value to what I have experienced, whether the audience is a single compassionate friend, a caring family member, a concerned pastor, a group of readers or conference attendees, or a lonely person in need of conversation. Instead of feeling isolated and alone, I identify with others as they identify with me.

God provides this same identification through His Holy Spirit. Jesus refers to Him as the *paraklete*, which comes from two Greek words – para (alongside) and kaleo (to call). Thus, the word means "one called alongside to help." No wonder He is also called the Comforter. The healing we experience in the very act of prayer is in part derived from knowing that God is listening; He is the sovereign audience.

Our hope for a legacy, and our desire to see others achieve a legacy, is so compelling that some have told their story only after death, either with their own diaries, such as Anne Frank, or through their loved ones, as Jim Elliot did through his wife, Elisabeth Elliot in her book, *Through Gates of Splendor*. The poet Gale Warner (*Dancing at the Edge of Life*) wrote several notebooks full of her stories as she was dying, finally to be heard and reproduced by those who wanted to hear her story. *Letters to Emily*, a fictional novel about a grandfather wanting to tell his story to his granddaughter as he was losing his ability to communicate due to progressive Alzheimer's disease, used a clever computer game of clues to beckon his family to uncover his story and to share it with Emily, his precious audience. This strikes a chord with parents and grandparents who desire to leave the legacy of their stories to the succeeding generation.

The spiritual implication of this benefit is illustrated by the Mosaic writings in the Old Testament. They contain the stories of the Israelites' experience, and transmit information about God's love, character, and moral code.

Friendships develop, sometimes imperceptibly, when one's narrative is shared. They occur with the stranger sitting beside you on the airplane, the classmate assigned to the adjacent seat, the other patients waiting in the doctor's office, the new member of the Bible study group, or someone else brought into the sphere of your life, when they share their unique story with you, and vice versa. Such relationships have evolved during my volunteer work at a guild serving blind people. Many of the participants in our "Tell Your Story" forums have come to the guild to learn job skills or to obtain rehabilitation for adapting to blindness. Because of the urban setting with its diverse immigrant populations, many have come to improve English skills, bringing with them the culture and the language of their native countries.

The original purpose of the "Tell Your Story" forum was to improve English skills through presenting simple information to each other in the group. Although many did not know each other in more than a cursory way, and were separated by language barriers, we saw strong relationships develop through the presentation of stories. Multiple factors that followed the stories built strong friendships. Shared experiences, emotional comfort, and advice-giving built bonds between the participants, and providing healing to the storytellers.

I wrote this book to underscore the importance of people telling their stories, and to free people to share their stories with others. I will touch on many areas of life, and offer sufferers a chance to share their stories. Some stories share information, give advice, or provide resources to help others. Other stories do not offer such concrete remedies. But the mere telling of a story, with the possibility of a shared experience between the teller and the listener, has genuine value.

In each of these narratives, biblical references introduce a faith perspective and, more importantly, challenge the readers and the groups that may be using this text to have biblically based discussions about the meaning of the narrative. In the end, the relationships arising from a "Tell Your Story" forum will strengthen all those who participate in the comforting work of the *paraklete*.

CHAPTER 1

BLESSED AND STRESSED TRANSITIONS
BY ELAINE LEONG ENG, MD

Let me stimulate ideas about narrative sharing by providing an example of a story. Your initial reactions to this story will help you understand the benefits of telling your story, whether it be connecting with one or more of the themes, or stirring up emotions you have felt. It might even prompt you to write or tell your own story.

"Are you all right?"

My college professor had scheduled a history class in a new location during the dark evening hours of late fall, and I was struggling to find the path that led to the door. None of the other students seemed to have any difficulty.

Embarrassed and confused, I said meekly, "No, I'm okay, Professor Gelfand." Then I followed him by listening to the sound of his footsteps. There were other times at Princeton when I had shied away from walking the dark campus at night for fear of falling into the lake or getting lost. I assumed that I was experiencing night blindness from a carrot-poor diet.

College is a proving ground, and Princeton was no place to do anything but excel. Any deficiency or limitation on my part would only be a source of weakness and shame. I paid no attention to it. After all, I was pre-med and preparing to answer God's call to pursue a career in medicine.

Four years later, graduation from the Albert Einstein College of Medicine culminated a sacrificial period of endless studies and led into the beginning of specialty training. I selected obstetrics and gynecology, a field I loved because it was a happy part of medicine to bring babies into the world, and I enjoyed working with women. Knowing that surgery was a big part of the field, I continued to ignore the night vision difficulties and assured myself that there would be no problems for me in the good lighting conditions of the hospital and office. Still, the tension of my aspirations clung to me as I embarked in my OB/Gyn training at Bellevue Hospital. Could my faith and trust in God, who had called me into this field, overcome the anxiety I felt about my adequacy for the work ahead of me?

During the Bellevue years, other demands and concerns rose to the forefront of my pressured and sleep-deprived mind. Married for five years to a Christian man, I always wondered how Cliff could put up with my consuming study and clinical rotation schedule all those years. I assumed that God had provided the right life partner, who seemed perfectly content to work and then watch television while I studied. He never complained. Our son, Brian came along just before I graduated medical school. Two years later, my daughter Genevieve arrived. In fact, the labor pains bringing her into the world began while I was on call at the hospital delivering other women's babies.

What a relishing time of rest I had when I called my covering doctor in to relieve me. I caught a few scenes from an Alan Alda movie before the pains intensified, and then Patty, my friend and chief resident, rushed me to the labor and delivery room of the hospital next door, just in the nick of time. Genevieve loudly announced that it was time for her to be born while the whole staff watched in stunned surprise. I had bypassed the labor and delivery rooms and found myself in the recovery room where the birth took place. I guess it was a shock for them that an OB/Gyn resident doctor and her superior couldn't get me to the hospital on time for a calm delivery. In retrospect, nothing in my life has been conventional.

Motherhood is God's most precious calling for women, I realized. Why was I being kept from this vocation by an equally compelling call? Distraught by my divided loyalties between career and motherhood, I found that I could not be fully happy at home or work. When I was at the hospital, I longed to be with my babies. The long hours at the hospital, being on overnight call every third night, and the long commute home made it impossible to see Brian and Gen for more than a few hours every other night. When I was at home, I would worry about my patients and the grueling schedule at the hospital. There was even less time for God, no room for leisure, and no time for my husband. Life evolved into a long list of responsibilities.

Then the specter of my night blindness revealed itself in full form. In 1983, I was diagnosed with retinitis pigmentosa, an inherited eye disease that would lead to progressive loss of vision. In fact, I had already met the legal criteria for blindness due to the tunneling down of eyesight typical of this disease. Teaching the interns and junior residents how to do deliveries and Caesarean sections, I found that I could not see clearly some of the things they were doing. I thought I just needed stronger glasses, but I found out it wasn't the case. I was going blind.

Once I learned the diagnosis, I knew that I could not ethically practice in a surgical subspecialty. I resigned the next day. Somehow, God made it possible for me to accept this news as I saw that it was not totally tragic. I was now permitted to devote myself to full-time motherhood, a role that was important not only to my mental well-being but to that of my children as well.

You can imagine the surprise of my ophthalmologist when I accepted my news with peace and calm. Judging by the look on his face and the reaction of the Bellevue OB/Gyn dept, this was a tragedy. But Romans 8:28 says: "And we know that God causes all things to work together for good to those who love God, to those who are called according to His purpose."

This so-called "tragedy" in my life brought good with it. I now had the opportunity to be a full-time mom to my babies and watch them grow while I still had some eyesight left. Those images and memories are permanently ingrained in my mind. Full-time parenting is a privilege that many of us sacrifice on the altar of our profession or ministries, but my illness afforded me the opportunity to lift that sacrifice from the altar.

Transitioning from doctor to Mom was more natural and enjoyable than I could have imagined, so that I call it the "blessed transition." I enjoyed every aspect of motherhood: feeding Brian and Gen, singing songs to them, teaching them, reading to them, and playing with them. I still had some eyesight left so these activities were possible. I also could see their little happy faces, images that are now ingrained in my memory as clear as a photo album.

A more stressed transition followed. After my youngest child entered school, I considered my professional goals. My ophthalmologist told me that there were two fields open to a blind physician: psychiatry and statistics. Since I hated math, psychiatry was the only option. With the advice and prayers of a pediatric colleague, I returned to training in the field of psychiatry.

The contrast between the fields of OB/Gyn and psychiatry was dramatic. I had not even taken one psychology course in college and had never focused on psychiatry in medical school. Moreover, the anxiety I now faced in training as a blind physician became daunting. Learning an entirely new body of clinical information and adjusting to the intricacies and challenges of doing it blind hurled me into a world of worry.

Groaning is an important part of prayer. The groans I could not articulate came with saying goodbye to full-time motherhood. The months prior to my start of the psychiatric training program were overshadowed by depression and pain. I felt the need to hold on harder to my school aged children, as if I were going to lose them, but I lacked the insight to understand this. So the groans written about by Paul in Romans 8:26-27 poured forth from my mouth as I asked the Holy Spirit to pray for me the words that expressed my trouble. The Lord knew what was bothering me even if I could not express it verbally.

My Lord remained faithful to me as I trained in the hospital. The department of psychiatry held preliminary discussions with residents as to whether they would want a disabled colleague. Most had hesitations, and one was vehemently opposed, but the department chairman went to administration and requested an extra slot for me, letting a "normal" person fill the original position. Hence I was the "extra help" rather than a burden who might not be able to hold her own. This made everyone accept my coming.

During my years at North Shore University Hospital, the faculty queried often as to how they could help me progress. I felt comfortable in tailoring my learning around my adaptive needs. Readers were hired. Office space was made handicap accessible. Consultation-liaison psychiatry, which required me to go to other wards in the hospital, was done with a partnering resident and not alone; he would read charts, and I would do the evaluation. In the process, I realized that I was teaching those around me what was best in the interest of my progress and adaptation. I knew I had to be articulate while maintaining sensitivity to the concerns of my fellow residents and hospital staff.

Professionally, as a psychiatric resident, I became a keen observer, and a student of the ranges of behaviors and reactions that others might have toward me. Personally, I did not want to be the entitled, demanding, helpless handicapped person. So the role of a teacher/collaborator with my colleagues allowed us to work successfully together. The team approach in the inpatient unit made it very congenial for such a mindset. The nursing and ancillary staff were vital and gracious in supporting my work as a resident.

Through discipline, I kept up my journal reading and read the standard psych texts already recorded in the Library of Congress.

My faith in God formed the conviction that I would succeed. During my residency, objective tests showed that I had started at the bottom, but by the end of four years had climbed to the top in terms of psychiatric knowledge. The process was clearly a group achievement supervised by the Lord. It taught me that much of what we do is dependent on others. The lack of sight just made this clearer to me, while other physicians felt compelled to "make it on their own." The quote "no man is an island" is a tough lesson for many doctors. I do not think I could have learned it so well without my blindness.

While I was learning all the medical information, I discovered that the Bible, particularly the book of Proverbs, contained important and reliable wisdom for counseling. I know that the Author of this book provided the circumstances, strength, and ability that allowed me to train and graduate successfully.

I have now been in practice for over twenty years, working and teaching at the interfaces of psychiatry, OB/Gyn, and Christianity. During these years God has blessed me with the privilege of publishing my writing and teaching my discovered understanding. My blindness and the challenges I have faced have taught me great lessons about dealing with anxiety and helping those who suffer from it. I shared this insight in my books such as *"Martha, Martha:" How Christians Worry,* and *A Christian Approach to Overcoming Disability: A Doctor's Story.* My opportunities to serve the Lord broadened with my involvement with the Physician's Resource Council at Focus on the Family. I also have been privileged to serve with many faithful healthcare professionals and educators in both the international and local arms of the Christian Medical and Dental Associations. Serving alongside so many Christian colleagues and friends has provided me with an extensive community within the body of Christ. God has brought me great satisfaction and gratification in my ministry, my career, and my family. My husband, Cliff, and I are very proud of the way our children have continued to develop into fine adults under our roof and God's care.

"What would happen if you could see again?"

This new question began to haunt me because its remote possibility has emerged. Why was I feeling this sense of unease when all my friends and family would rejoice in a cure? In the book, *A Christian Approach to Overcoming Disability: A Doctor's Story,* I describe the work of Dr. Alan Chow in creating an experimental "artificial retinal implant," so-called the "bionic eye," heralded as a potential treatment for patients with retinitis pigmentosa.

Might that be possible for me? Now at age 55, with children grown into wonderful adults, an established career, gratifying ministries, and now totally blind, what would sight offer? It's not as if the biblical "locusts" took years from my life. True, I lost my sight, but there has been nothing I have lost that God has not restored many times over in His amazing ways. Would my life change if I regained sight? Could I live in humble dependency on Him the way I have learned to do? Will people treat me differently or expect from me things that I never learned to do? It probably seems strange to you that I would have these worries, when most would expect to be jubilant if their sight were restored, but this paradoxical phenomenon has been described before.

However, when I realized that if I were to see again, I could hope to see the faces of future grandchildren, that was more than enough to quell any trepidation toward change for this potential grandmother. On April 18, 2009, I sat in the office of Dr. Chow, nestled in a delightful suburb of Chicago. My friend, Leslie, picked me up at the airport and drove me. She was not only my driver but also moral support and prayer partner for this venture. Friends had prepared me not to get my hopes up, as this was still experimental. I also knew that Dr. Chow's research, although promising, had had some setbacks both in financing and in getting necessary approvals for the next steps in making the bionic eye available for the market.

So now I faced the emotional roller coaster of hoping for a cure and coping with the fact that treatment may not work or even exist. Disturbing as this situation was, I bravely trouped into his office to face the verdict. After a few introductory remarks, Dr. Chow admitted to me that his research showed major improvements on his small series of human subjects. The improvement was dramatic in several cases, and these patients had been featured in a "Dateline" television program; but his work had been hampered by investments made on his research. Those funds were no longer available due to the economic downturn. Much time had been lost. He had reapplied to the FDA for approval to carry on his research, but he did not know when that might be granted. It could be a year or more, and it also could be never.

After examining me, he did say that if the implant device were approved, there was a reasonable chance it would improve my left eye. It's hard to know what to do with these mixed pronouncements of hope and frustration. The waiting process could be an arduous one. I suddenly felt like a patient with a chronic illness bordering on the cusp of living life only to look for a cure. This did not suit me well, as I was used to moving on to all the things God had enabled me to do. With a little resourcefulness, lots of help, and His abundant grace, life had moved along so well until this human promise of a scientific breakthrough that might not work out. This was tough. Why even raise hope? I was better off being blind and content.

"Are you all right?"

The speaker, Eric, kindly turned to me and asked the same question Professor Gelfand had posed so many years ago at Princeton. Plagued with a hacking cough that would not go away, I tried to suppress the commotion it was creating by drinking bottles of water and sucking on cough drops to no avail. He then said, "We're like family here. Let us know if you need help."

"I'm okay," I replied, not wanting to interrupt the flow of the meeting. Dr. Marcia Lucas and I had traveled from New York to Europe with a group of students from the Alliance Graduate School of Counseling to teach a course on counseling for global engagement. In one of our destinations, Eric's center invited us to learn about his work internationally. Integrating psychology with biblical teaching, Eric taught us his counseling model, "The Exchange at the Cross." He explained that much of this method involves telling your story of crisis, trauma, or loss in a safe and accepting environment over a period of time, long enough to share one's situation and bring it to the cross – where Jesus is present not only as the sin bearer but also the pain bearer. The prophecy about Jesus in Isaiah 61:1 states, "The Spirit of the Sovereign LORD is on me, because the LORD has anointed me to preach good news to the poor. He has sent me to bind up the brokenhearted, to proclaim freedom for the captives and release from darkness for the prisoners" (NIV).

So, to answer the question, "Am I all right?" Hope denied is like hearing that you have won a prestigious award or received a promotion at your job and then hearing that it was all a mistake. In the brief period between the mixed messages, your mind has created a new life for yourself that you now must surrender.

The potential of seeing future grandchildren, baby-sitting capably, and enjoying them fully transforms itself into the painful reality of relying on touch and sound. Only when they hold still can you connect with them, only to lose all contact when they move, even if it's just a few feet away. Panic and helplessness occur when the child has moved to a place where you cannot even see if he or she is safe. Babysitting alone without the help of others careful eyes is unlikely.

I did not feel this with my own children, partly because of God's grace in protecting me from such fears, but also because I had more vision then than now.

In a sense, I'm living out issues that I should have had earlier in life. The possibility of restoring my eyesight gave me the momentary dream of being more able to travel or walk along certain areas that have been restricted to me unless accompanied by a sighted guide. It also might enable me to avoid bumping into obstacles that produce the annoying bruises and scars that mottle my shins. Maybe I could wear shorts again without fear that others will think I've been abused.

The most crucial loss in this newly dashed hope has been a diminished sense of contentment and joy in receiving God's plan for me. My friends and I have always been amazed at how beautifully the Lord has enabled me to handle the challenges of blindness and to move on to a fulfilling career, family life, and ministry. We knew it to be God's grace and a divine gift. So this excursion into a brief hope brought me down to the world of suffering and loss that most of the world understands. Left to my desires, I'd prefer not to have the pain at all, but this trial, as those before it, has brought a good that God wants for me.

"The thief comes only to steal and kill and destroy; I have come that they may have life, and have it to the full," Jesus says in John 10:10 (NIV). In *The Exchange at the Cross* model, Eric asks, "What has the thief robbed from you in your loss?"

Hope, for one thing. This is not to say that Dr. Chow or another researcher will not eventually be successful in deriving a cure for retinitis pigmentosa. Since I don't claim to understand these areas, I choose not to think any further about them. The question at hand is, "What did the thief take from me?" Hope, contentment, and a resilient faith? Will this loss last?

As I was writing about the above question, I needed a mind and heart break. At this point, most folks at Eric's center would have spent a relaxing afternoon in the rustic mountainous area of the retreat site enjoying the views and fruit orchards and blue skies illuminating the lush valleys. With no eyes to view mountains, I found refreshment in a conversation with Linni.

Dealing with the long-term arduous treatments for multiple myeloma, a form of blood cancer with kidney complications, and a schedule full of chemotherapy, dialysis, and many hospitalizations, Linni paradoxically radiated a grace and contentment that had until now matched mine. While most would crumple from despair at the medical setbacks she experienced, Linni met each challenge with a matter of fact acceptance and a hope for God's grace to bring her through. Although a cure would be the hope, she simply took solace in each day as she found meaning in her walk with God and her daily routine. We both sang in the choir and from time to time would share how God had given His grace to us to accept our medical conditions. We were grateful that by some divine power we did not experience the full pain of our diagnoses.

She walked over to me after church to ask me a medical question about some recent symptoms. After answering her, I took the opportunity to ask her if she had ever looked at the losses in her life after her illness. I told her that in writing down my story at this stage of my life, I had been propelled into re-experiencing the losses in a new way. She remarked that when others have asked her to talk about having a serious and life changing illness, she was unaware of any depression or need to mourn, and she was perfectly happy to keep it that way.

I had to agree with her. That morning, I felt mired in sadness while intentionally counting the losses of my life due to blindness. The fact is, I had always been the type of positive person trained to "keep my thoughts captive." Let me just clarify that my successful adaptation to blindness is not due to any meritorious work on my part, but rather a miracle of God through His word and divine power. In addition, people who experience grief, sadness, and upset over major losses in their lives are no less spiritual in their Christian walks or applications of God's Word.

Yet the Bible contains remarkable truths, which form the basis for modern psychotherapeutic tools. My preferred treatment for anxiety is cognitive behavioral therapy (CBT). This form of counseling helps people maintain realistic truth based on good thoughts instead of anxiety-provoking or depressing ones. It is a great tool professionally and personally.

I could hear myself give the following lectures on CBT, integrating it with faith principles taken from Philippians 4:6-9 which states: "Do not be anxious about anything, but in everything, by prayer and petition, with thanksgiving, present your requests to God. And the peace of God, which transcends all understanding, will guard your hearts and your minds in Christ Jesus. Finally, brothers, whatever is true, whatever is noble, whatever is right, whatever is pure, whatever is lovely, whatever is admirable – if anything is excellent or praiseworthy – think about such things. Whatever you have learned or received or heard from me, or seen in me – put it into practice. And the God of peace will be with you" (NIV).

To my students, audiences, patients, and myself, at times, I would explain the seven coping skills taken from this passage. First, we must halt all anxious thoughts, as they, especially the repetitive catastrophic ones, do not get solved by over thinking them. Second, I'd ask the audience to turn their attention to something other than their anxiety thought, what is called re-focusing. Prayer and petition are vital to those who have faith in God to answer. Thanksgiving expressed by counting one's blessings, is a great mood enhancer, as one is forced to think about joyful things rather than dwelling on depressing thoughts. Realistic appraisal comes when one thinks about whatever is true rather than being mired by our worries and fear. Thinking about what is lovely such as God's creational scenery is far better than being locked in pessimism. Putting all these coping skills into a program of regular practice is what Paul prescribes in the last verse of this passage. Here we have divine CBT in a nutshell. Having been a practitioner of these skills in all spheres of my life has really helped me to overcome many of the hurdles that have come my way.

I am now facing a new transition in my career. My next call in medicine is the study of hospice and palliative medicine. Embarking on this new journey, I believe that having a chronic condition with no likely cure will help me understand how to help dying patients. Such patients need to consolidate their lives when they face the fact that all treatments for healing have been tried and have been unsuccessful.

The terminal phase of life is a time to consider what tasks must be accomplished in the dying process. Patients need to put their affairs in order, find meaning in the lives they've led, mend broken relationships, forgive others, obtain peace with God, and more.

So, with much trepidation, I tell my story and include what the thief has taken from me. First of all, the simple answers: sight and the privileges of vision are obvious. Appreciating the beauty of God's masterful work in all its glorious splendor can never be taken for granted. Secondly, I have lost the freedom of mobility. The mere act of driving myself to any desired place or taking public transportation without the stress of getting lost is something I no longer experience. That independence is hard to surrender. Many elderly parents experienced the same trauma when forced to give up driving. Third, especially for a woman, not being able to see as I try on clothing and make-up is a painful loss. I haven't seen myself in twenty years, so on my excruciatingly curious days, I find myself going through all sorts of contortions and angles in front of a mirror just to see if I can get a glimpse of one eye or my lips or even an impression of my hairdo – but to no avail. Also, not seeing my children's faces after the ages of nine and eleven leaves me guessing and somewhat worried that I might not be able to look at them and tell them with sincerity how adorable or attractive they are looking. *What will their sense of self be*, I asked myself in their teen years, *if I can't tell them.*

Naturally, I'm curious to know how my husband looks, too. While these are trivial external traits, and not nearly as important as their hearts and souls, not seeing their physical bodies still is a loss. Finally, the thief tries to steal my sense of self-worth and my sense of competence when I am dealing with a difficult clinical situation, or when I'm frustrated with something as trivial as the completion of an important form. I need help to perform some of the most simple functions.

All of these things are gone with the thief, but I'm glad to say that God has provided more than I could ever imagine in making up for the gaps. In fact, He has done so in such a way that the generous supply of friends and colleagues all around the world has extended my boundaries of love and ministry globally. When I take into account this gain in the midst of my loss, I realize I have less to nail on the cross for Jesus to bear than one would think. All that is left to nail on the cross is the work of Dr. Alan Chow and others working on a cure or treatment for retinitis pigmentosa, and the hope or lack of ever getting vision on this side of heaven.

Fortunately for me I am very task oriented, and find satisfaction in completing meaningful obligations or callings from the Lord. This gives me excitement to pursue the next calling in my medical career. Somehow He orchestrated my entering the study of hospice and palliative medicine two years ago. I don't know why He is doing this, but I'm beyond having to know everything before I do it. It is simpler to just obey. And, Lord willing, this will be completed by the end of 2011.

Ironically, it is a field where the compassionate care of the terminally ill affords me a chance to treat those to whom medicine has shut the doors on offering the hope of a cure. This resonates with the place where I might be in with my failed hope of a bionic eye. Remarkable are the ways God chooses to instruct us. In the end, all I may have lost in the journey of life is eyesight. Thankfully, eyesight is not the same as vision.

So I celebrate my journey in telling my story thus far with the song "Be Thou My Vision." In conclusion, whatever I have lost, whatever the thief has stolen from me, I have surrendered and exchanged at the cross for something even better. The list is hammered there for Jesus to bear. In retrospect, He has already borne much of it emotionally and eternally. My most important question is, "What have I received from Him in my so-called losses?"

Blindness is a weakness, but the Bible says that weakness in Christ is strength, so I have strength. As you can tell, He has given me accomplishments that no one blind or sighted person deserves; and so, I humbly bring these before Him as an offering.

There is no need to collect or display trophies where I am going. I have lost my eyesight, but He has given me vision as I sing "Be thou my vision, oh Lord of my heart, Naught be all else to me save that Thou art. Thou my best thought by day or by night. Waking or sleeping Thy presence my light."*

For a moment I had lost hope, but from the storehouse of the Lord, His abundant supply now fills me.

So thank you for listening to my story. Would you share yours? Perhaps some of the themes in my story resonate with those in your lives. Or my story may have triggered feelings that you have experienced at some point in your life story. Don't worry if you don't think your story is not as dramatic as the one I have told. Even though you may not be blind, even if you have not lost a child, even if you have not experienced extreme hardships, whatever your unique story, it will help others to hear, and it will help you to share it.

*Translated into English from ancient Irish text by Mary E. Byrne.

――――――――――――

Questions for personal reflection and/or discussion:

1. If you lost your sight, how do you think it would affect you – emotionally, relationally, spiritually?

2. If you have had a different loss that has affected you significantly, write it down in a journal (start a new one if you need to) and if possible, share it in a group setting.

3. Express in your own words what it means to you that in all things God is working for the good of those who love Him.

4. How do you think that prayer and dwelling on good things can affect your feeling of loss or grief? Read over Philippians 4:6-9. What does it say to your mind? What does it say to your heart?

5. To what degree is your personal faith helpful in times of loss?

CHAPTER 2

A SOFT BLANKET – A JOURNEY THROUGH LOSS*
BY RONDA KNUTH

"Comfort, comfort my people, says your God" (Isaiah 40:1, NIV).

One mother carries her longed-for baby to term, dreading, yet anticipating, the difficult labor to come. When her work is done, she holds the fulfillment of her dreams tightly in her arms. She counts tiny fingers and miniature toes, and plants tender kisses on baby's sweet nose.

Another mother labors in agony, torn, wanting the pain to end, knowing that when it does, the baby she has birthed will be lifeless and cold. She will hold, she will weep, she will unwillingly release.

One mother frets, not understanding the privilege of colic, sleepless nights, earaches, and runny noses. Another weeps for lost kisses, soiled diapers, first words, and skinned knees. I am that mother.

It has been twenty-two years since our son left the safety of my womb to be cradled in the arms of God. An ultrasound confirmed what the lack of movement caused us to suspect – our baby no longer lived. Not wanting to induce, the doctor advised us to wait for labor to begin spontaneously. So, we waited. We waited for one whole week.

Mere words cannot describe the torment and agony of those days spent waiting. My mother-heart ripped in two. Every time the baby's body shifted in me, I was convinced that the doctors had made a mistake, that our baby had not died. I convinced myself that in the end God would heal my baby and he would surprise everyone when he was born healthy and alive. I rode a roller coaster of emotion full of twists and turns.

Just two years earlier we had relinquished another child to heaven's care when Baby Knuth miscarried. My tormented mind struggled to accept the loss of another baby. As a committed Christian, I believe in the sovereignty of God. That belief brought me little comfort during the long, night hours. Perhaps it made my pain more difficult. I wrestled, questioning all I had ever learned about Him. "Why, God, why? Why won't you save my baby?"

With the onset of labor, my husband, Rob, and I made our way to Lutheran Hospital, and I settled into a bed in Labor and Delivery. A kind nurse, who had herself experienced a stillbirth, kept vigil with us. She sat unobtrusively close by ready to help should we need her, while allowing us privacy as I labored to bring this child into the world.

Unless you have been there, you cannot imagine the anguish of labor without the promise of life. The doctor predicted a speedy delivery, but he was wrong. The painful labor lasted for hours. When at last it was over, we held our tiny son in our hands and struggled to make sense of a loss that seemed so senseless. He was perfect in every way, except for the umbilical cord wrapped around his right leg. What possible good could come from this little one's demise?

We named him William Andrew Knuth, but I called him Billy. A week later, I stood beside the miniature, satin-covered white casket holding his body. I was numb with grief, spent to the very core of my being. If I survived, it would be because of the kindness of family and the grace of my God.

In my grief I questioned, *Do I have a right to cry for this child I never knew?* What to do with pregnancy loss was a mystery in those days. Some thought you should simply chalk it up to experience and move on. "You can always have another baby." Others were quick to offer pat answers designed to disallow the pain; for example, "God must have needed another little angel." Even a brazen few suggested, "This is punishment for your sin."

A nurse from the hospital called to say that photos taken of Billy had been lost. The one memento I thought we would have with which to remember him was gone. Now all I had were a few scant memories. In time, even they would dim. *Now that this crisis is over, will my baby be forgotten? Will anyone remember that he once existed?* I wondered.

Time brought little relief. My questions remained unanswered. The will to break loose from my despondency weakened with each passing day. I felt abandoned by God. I longed for a place of rest, a kind word, an understanding heart. Not knowing what else to do with the unrelenting pain, I wrapped it in a pretty package and stuffed it towards the back, on a shelf high in the closet of my heart. Then I shut the door and walked away.

Pretending it did not matter did not prevent my unresolved grief from exacting a ruthless toll. Depression became my constant companion. No one knew the depth of my pain, because I did not tell them. Some days I did well just to put one foot in front of the other.

Eleven years later, on a beautiful spring day in May, I stood before that door once more when I received an unexpected phone call. "Ronda, I have a friend whose baby was stillborn. I want to get her a gift. Do you have a suggestion?" Suddenly, the door of my heart swung open, and all the painful memories tumbled out. I was surprised at their intensity, and equally surprised at my ready reply, "Get her a soft blanket. One she can cuddle with and cry her tears into," I said. I knew that when her grief was spent, she would have a memento of her baby's brief life.

At first, the suggestion seemed surprising, perhaps even insensitive. *Why give a blanket that will never be used for the baby? Won't it remind the parents of their loss?* I wondered. Yet I knew from my own experience that such a loss is never forgotten. Neither should it be ignored.

There are many difficult aspects associated with pregnancy loss, not the least of which is coming home to a silent nursery with empty arms. Where a baby should be nestled there is, instead, nothing. Although I had not considered it before, I knew the suggestion I offered was right. Not only would the soft, cuddly blanket serve as a keepsake, but also it would fill empty arms – not with baby, but with something comforting.

"If I'd had a blanket like that," I told my friend before ending the conversation, "I know it would have been easier for me to grieve Billy's death."

A week later, I sat at the front desk at Sunrise Senior Living at Pinehurst, where I live out my love on a daily basis among a myriad of senior citizens. A quick glance at the clock told me that it would soon be time for the afternoon mail. I enjoyed the opportunity each day to greet the mail carrier. He had been delivering mail to my home for years, and now he was delivering it to my workplace. Usually our friendly exchange consisted of little more than a quick hello and maybe a bit of neighborly news.

But this day it was different. He laid the mail on the desk, then turned and placed a parcel in my hands saying as he did, "I thought you might like to have this now instead of waiting until you got home."

I could hardly wait for him to leave so I could examine the contents of my unexpected package. *I wonder who this is from?* The return label indicated an address in Ohio, and in an instant, I knew, without even opening the box, what was inside. What I did not know was the impact it would have on my life for years to come.

I removed the brown paper bag wrapping from the outside of the box, carefully loosened the covering, and peeked inside. The first thing I noticed was a piece of stationery folded neatly in two. Careful, lest it tear, I unfolded the paper and read the simple words it contained, "A blanket for William . . . for Momma. Trusting it's never too late."

Laying the note aside, I tenderly folded back the layers of crinkly, white tissue paper. Stifling a sob, I looked for the first time at the gift before me. With reverent awe, I extended a finger and felt the softness of a beautiful, pastel baby blanket. The downy blanket gave credence to the lives of baby Billy as well as Baby Knuth. It validated my losses and acknowledged the brief lives of my children. It seemed to whisper, "They haven't been forgotten." I wept then, blessed healing tears.

In time, I was able to do what previously had been impossible. I was able to release my babies back into the arms of God. Like Hannah of old, I could finally say, ". . . now I give him to the Lord" (1 Samuel 1:28, NIV). So profound was my healing that I knew I had to share it with others; thus, The Billy Blanket Project was birthed.

I learned of a certification program through a hospital in St. Charles, Missouri. The deadline had already passed when I picked up the phone and called. "Is there a chance you might accept me into the certification class?" With my name on the list, I tackled the next obstacle in my way. I needed $1,000.00, and we had $0. Word of my need spread among family and friends. Within one week, I had the necessary funds to travel from Denver to St. Charles and to pay for the certification.

Completing the class gave me the foundational information needed to adequately address the topic of pregnancy and early infant loss. Still I hesitated, wondering, *Will the gift of a blanket bring as much comfort to another grieving parent as it brought to me?*

I moved from questioning to action after the sensitive request of a close friend to receive the first blanket in memory of her two aborted babies. I presented it to her in December of 1998. The Billy Blanket Project was officially launched.

Limited finances were a challenge, but I prayed for provision. I found the second blanket at a local mall along with the tissue paper and gift bag – all on sale. The blanket went to the daughter of an area minister who had mentioned his daughter's miscarriage on the radio. I didn't know him, but I felt I should take a blanket by the church to give them for their daughter. The pastor's wife was at first a little skeptical, but was deeply moved by the gift, as were her daughter and husband.

Although the gift of a blanket may seem simple, it has a profound emotional impact. Many recipients weep tears of grief when they hold the blanket close. Some find comfort in sleeping with the blanket. Most find that it brings intense comfort. The gift of a blanket recognizes the brief life of their child with dignity and compassion. With my simple gift, I say to these hurting moms and dads, "I care. Your loss is valid. You need to grieve. It's okay."

One blanket went to Annie,* whose baby boy died soon after birth. Although Annie held her son wrapped in a blue blanket, she didn't get to keep it. When I sent her a handmade blue blanket, she responded with this note, "I found your package at the post office yesterday and cried as I read your letter and held on to this special blanket." Though it had been a number of years since her baby son had died shortly after delivery, the pain was still fresh. "It meant so much to be one of those who still needed a blanket … I was sure that I could tell my story and not cry anymore, but … no matter how you go on and heal, the deep pain is always there."

Annie in turn told me about Megan, a friend who had miscarried several years earlier. After I mailed her a blanket, Megan responded via e-mail, "Your gift was a wonderful surprise and so moving! I cried and cried. It really brought me back to my child that I lost …. It is so beautiful and soft. I will treasure it forever."

Megan later shared that for a period of time she slept with her blanket. One morning she awoke to find the blanket on her husband's side of the bed. Fathers grieve, too, but their grief often gets lost. After a pregnancy loss, the focus is on how the mother is doing, and a father tends to bury his grief because he thinks he needs to be strong for his wife.

Presenting a blanket to a mother, a father, and even the baby's siblings, acknowledges that grief is shared by the entire family. I know of one family who takes turns with the blanket depending upon who needs it most, whether Mom, Dad, or one of the children.

One especially moving story was told by Valerie. While getting ready for bed, she picked up the blanket so she could turn down the sheets. Overcome by a sense of her lost baby's presence, she held it to her breast, imagining that God was letting her hold her child. As she wept, her husband entered the room, and she turned away in embarrassment. Sensitive to the moment, her husband took her in his arms and said, "Can we lie in bed and hold her together?"

Whenever I learn of a grieving parent who has lost a baby through miscarriage, stillbirth, or early infant death, I want to give them a gift like mine. Not just any blanket, but a soft crib blanket, one that should have snuggled a baby but instead comforts a mother with empty arms or absorbs the tears of a grieving father. And, always I speak the words I wish had been spoken to me, "It's okay to cry."

My idea to soothe grieving hearts with comforting blankets quickly grew far beyond anything I had expected. Originally, my plan was that as moms came across my path, I would give them blankets. I didn't think it would get bigger than that. As people began to hear about what I was doing, however, I received calls requesting blankets for others. The concept expanded through word of mouth, e-mail correspondence, phone calls, and speaking engagements at local women's groups. The result was a ripple effect that I can only describe as, "One giving one, giving one, giving one."

I've given many blankets myself, and those who have themselves been given blankets have given countless others. Others who have heard of the blankets have given them to friends who have experienced pregnancy loss. Some have become involved by donating blankets or funds to purchase them.

Some wonder, "Is it such a good idea to give a blanket to the parents after a baby has died? Won't it remind them of their loss?" My reply is, "Do you really think they have forgotten?"

The ripple effect has taken blankets on missions to soothe broken-hearted parents from the Bronx in New York to comfortable Ranch Santo Margarita, California. They've winged their way to rural Humble, Texas, north to lazy Kimball, Nebraska, and even as far away as Germany. Other blankets have gone to a missionary, the wife of a popular talk show host, a sorrowing Lieutenant Governor and his wife, and a military couple miles from home. One mother wept when she received a blanket in memory of her son. Another young mom told me, "If I close my eyes and hold my blanket to my cheek, for just a minute its softness feels like my baby's face next to mine."

There's nothing magical about the blankets. The grieving parents will grapple with their own sorrow for a long time. They will have questions just as I did. They will wonder why a loving God allowed their baby to die. They will wrestle with Him, seeking to understand. There are no easy answers. I pray they will successfully navigate the turbulent waters of their own grief. And, I pray that when they are weary, and cannot run, they will rest in the Father's arms.

In the "Empty Arms, Aching Hearts" support group I offered at two different churches in the Denver area, I found the concept of the blankets to be valid. Once a week for eight weeks we gathered. We talked about pregnancy and early infant loss. We told our stories. We cried our tears.

One group was unique in that the very pregnant mother had not yet experienced the loss of her baby. The doctors had told Lana and her husband Roger that when their baby girl was born, she would not live more than a few minutes at best. They were convinced that they needed to carry her to term.

Near the end of the eight weeks, baby Myra was stillborn. Lana later shared, "I remember the night we received Myra's blanket. The hospital gave us a blanket for her, too. It was stained with her blood that she left behind as she lay on it for the pictures we now hold as one of few in a small box that does and doesn't contain her life. I hold the blanket you gave to us in advance of her death and remember its anointing and your prayer that the Holy Spirit would allow the blanket to comfort us in our remembrance of Myra. I know that prayer has been answered. I have slept with her blanket and felt God's peace cradle my wounded heart just as surely as I know that He cradles my daughter."

The members of Messenger class, a group Rob and I attend on Sunday mornings, have embraced the giving of blankets. Many times, after I've presented a need, they have "passed the plate" and collected the necessary funds to buy a blanket. They have experienced great satisfaction in partnering together to touch the wounded hearts of many.

Satisfying as well is the immediate transformation on the face of one receiving a comfort blanket. There's nothing like it. Knowing their baby has been remembered is priceless. Every time I hug a sorrowing father or wipe the tears of a grieving mom, I am reminded of the healing that began in my own life the day the mail carrier delivered my soft, pastel baby blanket. And, I am hopeful that through the gift of a blanket, they will begin a healing of their own.

In 2007, I felt the need to take a sabbatical from The Billy Blanket Project. Two years later, after being prompted by many, I took it out of sabbatical status. This time my role has changed from giver to teacher. Now, through public speaking and an instructional section at my ministry website *www.rondasrestingplace.net*, I teach others how to sensitively comfort others who are grieving by giving the gift of a blanket.

One recent evening while shopping at my local Walmart, I came across some incredibly wonderful, soft big-people blankets. Seeing them reminded me of two very special women I knew to be hurting. I guess I've known since taking the Billy Blanket Project out of "sabbatical status" that it was only a matter of time before my passion for giving a comfort blanket would enlarge to embrace not only those experiencing pregnancy or early infant loss – but to other hurts as well.

I purchased two blankets, along with lovely gift bags and tissue paper. One blanket went to Sue, a young mother of three who recently lost her husband to cancer. Within two months of his diagnosis, he was gone. At an area Concert of Prayer, I slipped in beside her and pulled her close. I wiped her tears with my thumb, and listened as she shared her heart. She wept as she told how so many, not knowing how to comfort her, have simply pulled away.

I wished for words to take the pain away, but there aren't any. She will have to walk this path of sorrow to its end. As she makes that journey, she will have a tangible reminder of my love for her in the soft blanket I gave her.

The other blanket went to Kate, a woman I work with who underwent chemotherapy, after having lost her breast to cancer. This was a very frightening time for her. She did not know Christ, so my genuine desire was that the blanket would be a catalyst for softening and opening her heart to the One who can give her peace on her journey.

It's always difficult when we meet sorrow face-to-face. Some choose not to go there for fear of saying or doing the wrong thing. The only thing worse than going through a traumatic event is going through it alone.

You may not know what to say or do, but you can give a soft, comforting blanket. You can say, "I'm sorry. I care. I love you." You'll be surprised what the simple gift of a blanket will do for one who is hurting.

Along with the blanket, I send a short note. I sent the following letter to Kate. Maybe it will stir your heart and provide some ideas of what to say in a similar situation:

Dear Kate,

Word on the street is that the next thing in line for you is chemo. I wish, I wish, I wish, I could spare you that journey. This has to be scary for you. Any time we face the unknown it's rather frightening and intimidating.

Remember one of the earliest video games to be released to the marketplace, named Pac-Man? There was a little round faced man that ate up ghosts in his way. When you have your treatments, think of your chemo as that little round faced man eating up the cancer.

Kate, there have to be moments when you feel so alone. Much as those of us who love you would like to take this from you, we cannot. I want you to know that I care, that you matter to me, that I am praying for you. You've read my story and you know that life has not been easy. I've found great solace in leaning on God. While He has not spared me the difficult ventures, He has walked them with me every step of the way. That is what I am praying for you, and will ask others to do as well . . . to pray that God will walk this with you all the way. When you think you can't go on, turn to Him and let Him carry you. He will, my friend. If you ask Him, He will.

There is a whole piece of my own journey that you know nothing about. One day I will share it with you. Just suffice it to say that this gift comes to you out of my own encounter with deep pain. It was a source of comfort and the catalyst for my own emotional healing. When you are tired, when you are scared, when you feel alone, wrap yourself in this gift and know that you are loved. Deeply loved.

I love you, my friend.
Ronda

I cannot help all those who grieve in the world, but I can help a few of them find the healing love of Christ tucked inside a soft, warm blanket. So can you, if someone you know needs a soft blanket to cry into.

*Cases are true, names are fictitious

Questions for personal reflection and/or discussion:

1. Grief is one of the most personal, painful, lonely experiences we will ever have. Using the feeling list below, circle five emotions you had immediately after your most significant loss to date:

love anger loneliness confusion hurt guilt shyness embarrassment fear caring jealousy understanding worry warmth patience excitement hate sadness sympathy moodiness shame gloom discouragement encouragement

2. What has been the most difficult aspect of grieving for you?

3. Describe how your loss has affected your family, your spouse, your children, your friends, and your relationships with them.

4. Talk about your relationship with God during this time of grieving. Have you found it easy to tell Him your hurt? Difficult to pray? Have you experienced moments of anger, which you have directed toward Him? If so, what can you do about it?

5. Share about someone who comforted you in an especially meaningful way. What did they say or do that helped?

CHAPTER 3
WHEN GOD & CANCER MEET*
BY LYNN EIB

It was 1990, and I should have been the picture of wellness. I was thirty-six, happily married with three wonderful daughters. I didn't smoke or drink and had been exercising several times a week for years. My eating habits characterized me as a "health nut." I looked fine, felt fine, but I was slowly dying inside. I had colon cancer, and of course, all cancers are fatal if left untreated. I thought the occasional blood was from a hemorrhoid and the irregular bowels from something I had eaten. My family doctor wasn't worried – why should I be?

On June 27, 1990, my wonderful world came crashing down. I can still see my husband's ashen face as he stood at the end of the hospital gurney while the gastroenterologist delivered the news of a cancerous tumor. I knew this was his worst nightmare revisited as his first wife had died of ALS (Lou Gehrig's disease) in 1971 when they were newlyweds. Surely this could not be happening again . . . but it was.

I had surgery a few days later to remove the tumor. If the cancer had been caught in the earliest stage, my chance of recovery without further treatment would be nearly 100 percent. At that point, I had been a follower of Jesus for seventeen years, and my pastor-husband and I had faithfully served the Lord throughout our then – sixteen years of marriage. Surely God would end this nightmare with a good pathology report. But He didn't. The report showed that the cancer had spread to the lymph nodes. I needed chemotherapy and possibly radiation; my chance of survival had dropped to maybe 40- or 50-percent. The thought of my husband being widowed again and not seeing my daughters, ages eight, ten, and twelve at the time, grow up was more than I felt I could bear.

I remember a friend came to my hospital room and told me God was going to teach me great things through this trial. I wanted to take the I.V. out of my arm, stab it in hers, and tell her, "You get in the bed and learn great things from God this way, because I don't want to." Instead, I just smiled weakly.

I was bolder with God (I figured He could read my mind anyway!) and told Him that I didn't want Him to eventually make something good come out of this, as I knew the Bible promised He could. Instead I wanted Him to take it all away. "And don't think you're going to pull me through this and I'm going to go and minister to cancer patients, because I'm not going to do it!" I told God with no uncertainty from my hospital bed. I think He might have smiled at me the same way knowing mothers do with rebellious toddlers at bedtime.

Three weeks after surgery, I started what was scheduled to be a year's worth of weekly chemotherapy with Dr. Marc Hirsh, an oncologist a few miles from my south-central Pennsylvania home. I actually had been sent by my surgeon to another oncologist, but chose instead to be treated by Marc because I knew of and greatly appreciated his strong spiritual faith as a Jewish believer. Little did I know what far-reaching and life-changing effects that choice would have on my life.

By the time I started treatments about a month later, I had become more accepting of what was happening. Besides, the chemo nurse explained to me that the side effects associated with the three drugs I was receiving were relatively mild and would take weeks to be felt. I counted people in sixteen states praying for me. Surely the treatments would go easily for me. But they didn't. The side effects started with the first treatment, and some were so strange they were barely mentioned in the oncology books.

My eyes watered profusely, my nose ran constantly, water tasted like chemicals, and I was nauseous twenty-four hours a day (the only anti-nausea medicine available at that time made me sleepy, and I couldn't function to take care of my children, so I rarely took it). On some days the air smelled so sickening I had to hold my nose when I was outside.

I was allergic to the main drug I was receiving, and the palms of my hands and soles of my feet turned flame red and felt like they were on fire. On some days I couldn't bend my fingers and had to walk on the sides of my feet. "Why isn't this easier?" I moaned to God, much like the Israelites did while wandering in the desert.

I now believe that God was allowing me to suffer so I could minister to suffering people.

Marc suggested I stop the treatments at six months instead of a year. I didn't argue.

I finished my treatments in February 1991, and I went back in May for my first check-up. I was the only one in the chemo room that day not getting chemo. I kept thinking how happy I should feel, but I didn't. I was overcome with sadness for the other patients, and I began to quietly weep. I wanted to take away their pain, but I couldn't. I wanted to give them peace, but I couldn't. Then the Lord spoke to my heart and said, "But you know the One who can, and you can tell them about Me."

"But I just want to put all this behind me and go on with my life," I argued. "Besides, I don't want to hang around people with cancer. It will be depressing. They'll die, and I can't take it."

Then, a few weeks later, I had a great idea. If I start a cancer support group, God will have to let me live because everyone will need me. But God reminded me that He doesn't make deals. I knew God was calling me to minister to cancer patients and I would not have peace until I obeyed, so in October 1991, I rather reluctantly started a Cancer Prayer Support Group with four people at the first meeting. My intent was to have a one-hour, once-a-month meeting. *That shouldn't be too depressing*, I thought.

Just to make sure it wasn't depressing, I decided to start off each meeting with jokes. I usually said something like, "I know cancer isn't funny, but you may not have had anything to laugh about lately, and I hope these jokes might bring at least a teeny smile to your face because I believe the Proverb that says "a cheerful heart makes good medicine."

Because I called my group a Cancer Prayer Support Group, I thought it would be a shame if someone came and left without getting prayed for, so we closed the meeting by holding hands, and I prayed by name for everyone there.

I could quickly see the people coming to the group needed more support than one hour a month and, strangely enough, I felt better after the meetings, instead of worse. We started meeting twice a month, and I became intimately involved in these people's lives. Our group continues to meet to this day and is as far as I know the oldest, continuously meeting Christian-based cancer support group in the country! We still start with jokes and snacks and finish up with prayers, as many around the circle pray for each other and thank God for His healing touches.

In July 1995, on the fifth anniversary of my cancer surgery, I stood before my church family and gave a testimony of what God had done in my life through my cancer experience – how the support group had given me great joy, how Marc and his wife had become very close friends with my husband and me – including prayer partnerships where our husbands have prayed together weekly, as have Elizabeth and I. I concluded my sharing that day with one small sentence: "Someday I hope I can quit my job and minister full-time sharing God's Word, peace, and love with cancer patients."

I knew it was a very unrealistic wish – there was no way I could quit my part-time public relations job and volunteer. We needed the money from my work, especially since our oldest daughter would be starting college the next year. But I couldn't deny it was a desire of my heart, so I secretly prayed that God somehow would make it happen.

There is a verse in the New Testament, Ephesians 3:20, which says God is "able to do exceeding abundantly more than we can ask or think. . . ." Less than a year later, that verse became true in my life in an amazing way.

Marc called and said he and Elizabeth wanted to talk with my husband and me about a "business proposition." I couldn't imagine what it could be. (Shaklee? Amway?) When we met, Marc said they had been praying about something for quite a while and felt it was the right time to ask me. He proceeded to offer me a job in his office as a Patient Advocate, who would minister to the emotional and spiritual needs of his cancer patients. Whatever I was paid at my present job, he would match. Needless to say, my tears flowed as I realized how God was answering my secret prayer.

So May 1, 1996, we began this new venture. We knew of no other physicians with a Patient Advocate, and according to folks at the Christian Medical and Dental Associations, there are only a handful of such positions in the country now. I don't know if any of them function as I do in our office, but my job description says that I will provide emotional and spiritual care for patients and their families/caregivers through verbal and written encouragement, emotional support, and spiritual intercession.

We initially tried to find someone else who had a similar position so we could model mine after it. But we could find none, so we simply "made it up" as we went. I greet every new patient to our practice and stay with them during the majority of their first visit to help them get comfortable with their surroundings. (I stay the whole visit if they're alone.) Patients and family members can talk privately with me in my office or chat with me as I wander through the chemo room. I also try to encourage patients through written notes, phone calls, hospital visits, and home hospice visits. Our well-stocked lending library offers inspirational books, as well as those on the topics of suffering, healing, caregiving, nutrition, laughter, and coping with treatment.

I keep Marc informed about any special emotional or spiritual needs in patients and help him to see how the world looks from their perspective. I often function as a liaison, helping to improve the doctor-patient relationship. But the main relationship I hope to improve is a patient's relationship with his/her Creator.

I've seen patients who were far from God brought near; patients who were alienated from God, reconciled; patients who were close to God shown how to really trust Him; patients who got miraculous healing; patients who learned how to get to heaven; patients who never had had anyone pray with them before; patients with bad news who found hope; and patients with good news who praised God. I'd like to introduce you to a few of these patients:

Meet **Alice** who was far from God when I first met her as a sev-

47

enty-nine-year-old woman with metastatic colon cancer. She was a delightful lady, who dressed and looked a lot like Granny Clampett from the *Beverly Hillbillies* TV show.

Alice usually felt she didn't fit in places, especially churches, because she felt she wasn't "good enough" by society's standards. But I was able to share with her that God loved her exactly the way she was.

She didn't like being around people that much, but she began regularly attending my support group and then my church until one day she confided that I was her "very best friend in the whole world."

Before her eventual death, she told me several times, "I love God and am ready to go home."

I believe God gave Alice a special healing that money could not buy.

I'd like you to meet **Vicki**, a fifty-six-year-old woman with recurrent leiomyosarcoma who wasn't only far from God, she was very alienated from Him and anything to do with faith.

When I first met her in our office, she indicated on her health history questionnaire that she had no religion, and spiritual faith was not important to her.

First, I began visiting her when she was in the hospital; because she was so desperate, she even let me pray with her. Soon she came to my support group, and eventually she shared with me she had been hurt by an incident at a church decades ago.

"I never really meant to stop going; it just happened," Vicki said.

When I shared the gospel with her, she said she wanted to think some more about such a momentous decision. In May of 2003 she finally visited my church, weeping as she came in the door.

Two weeks later, when an 86-year-old guest preacher declared that, "You belong to God and you need to give yourself to Him," Vicki was in tears again as she walked to the front, surrendering her life to the Lord.

At a later support group meeting, she shared, "I can't imagine what my life would be like without Lynn and Dr. Hirsh and God."

I'd like you to meet **Joe**, a man in his 70s with recurrent colon cancer, who was very religious, but had no assurance of heaven. As we talked one day at the local hospital, he firmly asserted, "I'm getting ready to die, and I'm trying to get my affairs in order."

We discussed all the practical matters involved in such a situation and then he added, "I'm trying to remember all my sins. I hope I haven't forgotten any."

I shared Scriptures with Joe about sin and forgiveness, reminding him that "Jesus paid the price for our sins"– the ones we remember and the ones we don't. I shared some more verses on God's assurance of eternal life, and we prayed together reaffirming Joe's trust in Christ alone.

A respiratory therapist came into the room for Joe's scheduled breathing treatment, but Joe said he felt so good he didn't need one right then.

"I can't tell you how much better I feel," Joe told me. "I felt better as soon as you came in the room. I feel like I could get up and dance!"

He asked me to come back the next day and read some more to him, but that never happened, because the next morning, at 4 AM, Joe passed away.

I could scarcely believe it. And then I thought to myself, *So that's what the forgiveness of God feels like for someone. That's what someone looks like when they know they're going home.*

I'd like you to meet **Huberta**, who, less than twenty-four hours after I met her wanted to know how to get to heaven. Huberta, or "Bird" as she preferred to be called, was in her early 50s, recently diagnosed with an inoperable lung mass. She was an emotional wreck the first time I met her and could scarcely stop crying.

The next day she came back to our office and wanted to chat with me, still twisting a crumpled tissue and dabbing her teary eyes. I had no idea what she wanted to discuss, but she quickly turned the conversation to spiritual matters.

"I don't know how to get to heaven," she admitted.

She started telling me about her life and some of the wrong

things she'd done. She added that some of her friends told her not to worry because these hadn't really been sins. But she and I both knew better. I explained the gospel to her, and she eagerly listened to and agreed with every word I shared. I didn't want to be pushy, but finally couldn't help but ask, "Would you like to pray and receive God's gift of eternal life?"

Bird immediately fell to her knees, weeping and clasping my hands as we prayed together. Several months of chemo followed that prayer, but the cancer was relentless and spread to her spine, paralyzing her from the waist down.

It wasn't long before Bird went on hospice, and I started visiting her each week at home. One day I noticed that she seemed to look different. "Why do you look so beautiful today?" I asked her.

"I'm at peace," she said. "On Sunday night this peace just came over me, and it hasn't left. It's incredible. It's so beautiful. I never thought I could feel this way!"

I'd like you to meet **Howard**, who only agreed to come and see me because his nurse-daughter insisted he needed to. Howard was in his early 50s with throat cancer, which required a total laryngectomy. He also was very depressed. In my office, I asked him if he knew what he was most depressed about, and he mouthed the word "DEATH."

He was so scared to die because he felt God was angry at him, and this cancer was punishment for a divorce many years before. I told him how that if he wanted to know how God felt about him and his cancer, he should know that, "God loves you and He weeps for you." Howard wept through our entire first talk that day and left with a copy of my just-published first book, *When God & Cancer Meet.*

A week later he showed up at my book signing at our office. He started to cry again, but this time they were tears of joy as he hugged me and thanked me for the book. "Your words helped so much. I am headed in a whole new direction," he said, as he showed off how he'd learned to speak by placing his finger over the hole in his throat.

At his next appointment, Howard told me he gave "God all the credit" for how he felt. When his wife bought him a golden retriever, Howard promptly named her "Faith."

I'd like you to meet **Darlene**, a forty-year-old with advanced liver cancer, who discovered that salvation is a free gift. I visited with Darlene in the hospital during her in-patient treatment, and after I prayed with her, she asked me, "Does Dr. Hirsh know you do this – does he know you talk about Jesus?"

I assured her that not only did he know – this is exactly what he pays me to do!

"Isn't he Jewish?" she queried, which led me to share Marc's story of how he came to faith in Jesus as his Jewish Messiah.

After her second round of chemo, Darlene said, "I feel the presence of God right here in my room."

After the third round, she cradled the paperback Bible I had just given her, while acknowledging that she had never read the Bible before and had no idea where to start.

A few weeks later, when I asked her what she had learned from reading the Bible, she said, "I never knew salvation was a free gift. I always thought you had to earn it."

A few months later Darlene said she had an important question to ask me. "When I die, I want to have a memorial celebration because I'm going to heaven – will you talk at it? – about me and the things we've talked about?" she asked.

"I would be honored to talk about you and the way you have come back to God through your cancer ordeal," I told her.

"Faith and prayer are all I have," she added.

Ten days later I stood in a packed room full of leather-clad bikers and told them that I believed I was special in Darlene's life for one reason – that I had shared the most special thing in my life – my relationship with Jesus Christ.

Darlene's friends took her ashes-filled urn for a "last, great" ride on a Harley, but I knew her best ride was the one that took her home straight to the arms of her waiting Savior.

I'd like you to meet **Millie**, a Jewish woman in her 80s, who said my first prayer with her was unlike any other she ever heard. Millie had been coming to Marc for many years before I started working for him, and I was anxious to meet her. As I walked over to her hospital room to make my introduction, I reminded myself to be especially sensitive to her beliefs. I certainly had no intention of mentioning Jesus.

However, we'd only been chatting a few moments, when Millie shocked me by saying, "I've been thinking that Jesus might be the Messiah. What do you think?"

I immediately changed my mind about not mentioning Jesus and began to share my story with her. She listened intently, and before I left, I asked and received permission to pray with her.

When I finished, she had a look of total amazement on her weathered face. "That was unlike any prayer I've experienced before," she said. "I felt the presence of God come over me as you spoke. Why doesn't it feel like that when I hear the rabbis pray?"

I told her I didn't know the answer to that question, but I knew that the presence she had felt was the power of the Holy Spirit touching her.

Our talks continued over the ensuing months, and I knew she was reading the Jewish New Testament I had given her. One day a hospital dietitian also shared her faith with Millie and when she asked her if she wanted to pray to receive Christ, Millie quickly replied, "I already have."

I'd like you to meet **Jackie**, a very strong Christian who thought perhaps she was doing something wrong when God didn't heal her as she was sure He would. Through our talks, prayers, and books I shared, she came to realize that while God is a healing God, but He doesn't always physically heal in the here and now.

At one particular visit, I knew she was going to get more bad medical news, so I offered to sit in while she met with the doctor and take notes so she and her husband didn't have to concentrate too much on all the medical details. It was quite an emotional time as Jackie, her husband, and I all were brought to tears with the latest medical blow.

But a few days later a note came to Marc from Jackie: "I had to write and thank you on behalf of Mike and myself for the way you handled our meeting yesterday. We so appreciate your straightforward, yet sensitive way of presenting the facts. To have Lynn there was a bonus blessing. Thank you for not rushing us and especially for initiating the time of prayer. We were going to ask, but you beat us to it."

What a privilege to walk with sisters and brothers in Christ through deep waters and allow them to feel God's presence through us. What more can I say? I do not have time to tell about **Susan** who saw God conquer her depression. About **Barbara** who has seen God's promises come true in her life. And about **Charlie**, a Jewish man who, after nearly ten years of our chats and support group meetings, came to know Jesus as his Messiah.

I am so thankful to have a job that allows me to give ultimate hope to patients. Many things are offered to them that provide temporary hope – traditional medicine, alternative treatments, and even experimental therapies. But temporary hope is in the things of this world. Ultimate hope, I believe, is in God through Jesus, His Messiah, and it is only ultimate hope that will give true peace.

And now you've seen a glimpse of what can happen when one doctor desires to see the kingdom of God established in his life and his practice, and when one hurting person (me!) allows God to have His way in her life and follows a path she originally thought she never wanted to travel.

God did not make a mistake in my life twenty years ago when He said no to my prayer for instantaneous physical healing. He had a much better plan for my life, and for that I am eternally grateful.

*This is the title of Lynn Eib's first book: *When God & Cancer Meet* (Tyndale, 2002). Available wherever books are sold.

Questions for personal reflection and/or discussion:

1. If you know someone close (relative, friend, or even yourself)

who has had cancer, what were the initial reactions of the various people involved: the patient, family members, friends?

2. Do you think that dealing with this diagnosis is easier or harder for believers?

3. Review Lynn's own journey with God and faith in relation to her own diagnosis. What surprised you? What impressed you? What encouraged you?

4. In relation to other kinds of losses that we can experience, loss of our health is right near the top for most of us. If you were faced with a loss of health diagnosis, would you find it easier to deal with if you had someone like Lynn to support you? If so, why?

5. Can anyone develop the characteristics that would make oneself a true encourager, as Lynn is? If so, what are three or more steps to learning how to help others in significant distress?

CHAPTER 4
FOXHOLE BUDDIES
ANONYMOUS

In the setting of war, a foxhole is a small pit dug by a soldier in a battle area to provide immediate refuge and shelter during enemy fire. If that space is shared by two soldiers, these warriors refer to one another as a "foxhole buddy."

In a poignant poem written by Penny Rock in 1968, one's deep commitment to a "foxhole buddy" is beautifully articulated using the following phrases: "until death do us part . . . for us it's an unspoken vow in war . . . the bond is not created out of passion, but by fear and need . . . I'll stay awake so you can rest . . . you'll give me food to keep my strength . . . I'll walk ahead to show you the path . . . you'll hold the light so I can see . . . I'll take the bullet so you can live . . . you'll cover my face to show respect . . . we are foxhole buddies tied to each other by endless trust and bottomless faith."

In the setting of everyday life, and especially in times of great challenge or difficulty, we need at least one "foxhole buddy" – that person who will stay by your side, despite the often unpleasant circumstances that might arise, and permit you to share your struggles honestly without judgment or condemnation. A foxhole buddy is one who is relationally committed to the other without reservation even when they know who – at the depth of your core – you really are.

During a season of unrelenting war for my marriage and family, I was most privileged to have three foxhole buddies. These amazing women, even while knowing the very real and ugly truths about me, my husband, my nuclear family, and marriage, stayed beside me in the foxhole during intense battle. Though the enemy of my soul was constantly firing deadly weapons at me and my family, my buddies did not abandon me. Instead, they authentically loved, listened, counseled, and prayed earnestly with and for me. Since the reciprocal relationship of a foxhole buddy is intensely loyal and founded on trust, there is also freedom to correct, advise, and rebuke in truth and love.

Without my foxhole buddies during my war, I am certain I would have at least surrendered to the enemy eager to devour me, or surely died on the battlefield. When I wanted to give up on my marriage and family, they would listen to and love me, and sometimes they would talk, but they never left me. When I needed to cry, they offered their time and energy to just be there, and helped carry the weight of circumstances that held me down. When I needed rest and refuge, they would offer practical help such as watching my children. These women and I have been mutually dedicated to one another, and we are trustworthy fellow warriors, sharing the load of one another's burdens even unto this day.

Specifically, my battle was to honor my marriage commitment. I have been married for twenty-one years – the first nineteen having largely been unbearably miserable and painful. Admittedly, however, there have been ebbs and flows of happiness mixed with occasional joy, such as the privilege of becoming parents to three incredible children.

What I did not realize on the day I pledged to remain married to my husband until death parted us, was that he would bring with him a beast that would wedge a chasm in our union. Within two months of our blissful wedded journey, I accidentally happened across the monster I would fervently fight for the next nineteen years – pornography addiction.

At that time, I did not realize the death grip this beast held on my husband's heart, mind, and soul. Nor could I understand why he chose not to fight it. Perhaps he felt utterly powerless to walk away from something that gave him momentary pleasure but ultimately resulted in long-term strife, grief, shame, and guilt. His addiction birthed enormous marital friction, extreme selfishness, job losses, and physical and emotional separation from his family.

To be fair, it is important to point out that my often grotesquely prideful, angry, embittered, and hateful reactions significantly added depth and breadth to the ever-growing crevice between us. Suffice it to say that for the first nineteen years of marriage, we fought in a relentless battle for ourselves individually, our marriage, and our three children.

Pornography addiction was as foreign to me as communicating in Portuguese. In my mind and thinking it seemed that all that he needed to do was "grow a backbone," gain willpower, walk away, say "no," and be done with it. Such a determined mindset worked well for me, so how could it be that difficult for him? Sometimes I wish my simplistic thinking was curative! Honestly, in many regards, any addiction is still an extrinsic concept to me.

Because I do not have an addictive personality, I do not comprehend why or how someone chooses a "drug" that is ultimately far more destructive than the temporary pleasure it may deliver. Thus, I was fighting something I knew nothing about with the only tools that had worked well for me in my past – relentless determination, pleading, persistence, withholding my love and affection, giving advice, trying to fix the problem, and, at times, simply giving up.

Yet, I do comprehend pain – be it physical, emotional, or mental – it hurts, and sometimes a lot! I now understand that addicted people live with frequent agony that they treat with their drug of choice. None of us wants to experience unpleasant things, so we learn ways to cope or acquire methods to numb the affliction rather than feel it.

I had no idea of the depth of the immense emotional pain my husband experienced, nor did he. All he knew was that pornography gave him pleasure for a time while taking away discomfort he could not even initially identify or articulate. In retrospect, he would also acknowledge feeling a sense of power and entitlement, but he was always seeking something more, yet he was never satisfied. Ultimately the seasons of using pornography reinforced, strengthened, and created a perpetual downward spiraling cycle that was constantly gaining momentum and control over him, and thus our marriage and family. The beast was becoming even more forceful and deadly as it gripped and conquered every realm of his being.

Simultaneously, the chasm that existed between us grew. Each of us became increasingly more selfish, distant, and independent from each other. In most cases, we communed only long enough to parent and cohabitate, which we mostly did well. We were masters at playing the game of looking great on the outside, performing good deeds, attending and being actively involved in church weekly, parenting and raising wonderful children. All the while, however, we were dying slowly and miserably on the inside.

Eventually the cracks in the cistern began to leak, and the stagnancy of our reality was becoming apparent to others. With tremendous shame and guilt, my husband confided in a close friend and our pastor. With enormous embarrassment, I did the same. While exceptionally difficult, shining the light of truth into that deeply vulnerable, personal, and intimate area of our lives and marriage commenced the healing process. I am compelled to point out that the journey has been a marathon, not a sprint. The initial revelation to our entrusted friends and pastor occurred in the fifth year of marriage.

I could write an entire book on the lessons this journey has taught me and those that ultimately healed me, my husband, and my family. However, if I were to boil all of them down into a single common denominator, it would be this – a devoted relationship with Christ is the only source of peace, hope, and healing for our dying souls. If you or I turn to any other fountainhead, we will be sorely disappointed and remain broken and hopeless.

As well, we were not created to be solitary travelers on the road of life. We were meant to be social creatures with a need to interact with one another – to share in the joys as well as in the burdens. That said, however, we are also warned in Matthew 10:16 to be, "as shrewd as snakes and as innocent as doves." In addition to being a valuable lesson I most often learned the hard way, what this Scripture has meant to me is that I need to be wise, not prideful, in choosing the companions whom I permit to share in carrying the load of my burdens.

Christ, the Almighty, modeled this to me in His own life and teaching. I can find several examples of Him interacting with, feeding, and teaching the masses. In other instances He is relating with several people, yet the numbers are significantly smaller by comparison. As depth of relationship is noted, I see that the numbers further decrease to the twelve disciples. Yet, in Mark 14: 32 – 41 the Bible teaches that even more intimate are three of the twelve, Peter, James, and John. It is these three men that accompany Him to Gethsemane just before He is to be betrayed and crucified. Despite the depth of authentic relationship with them, at Gethsemane there is still a time when Christ withdraws to commune with His father – alone.

In my journey of healing I have had the masses – my church, a network of friends, and coworkers. I also let in several people in my life who were very meaningful to me such as my trusted friends and family. Closer to me still, and similar to Christ's twelve disciples, were select friends and family who loved me dearly and knew some of my situation more deeply. My "three," literally and figuratively, are my foxhole buddies, noted above, who resided in the pit with me during the fiercest battle for myself, my husband, my marriage, and my family. They have never betrayed or abandoned me.

However, irrespective of their devotion to me, like Christ I had to leave them to walk further into my own "Gethsemane" and commune alone with my Father. Why? Only the triune God is the source of all hope, healing, courage, and strength. Like Christ in Gethsemane, the three did not and could not walk with me for a distance. While I was in solitude with my Father, like Peter, James, and John, they prayed.

I know my foxhole buddies were appointed to and accepted the call to walk my journey with me, and it exhausted them as well. I know they felt frustration, weariness, and fatigue that they could not fix my problem. But they trusted the Father's perfect will for me to "drink from the cup" that God permitted in my life and marriage. They believed that God had a bigger purpose for me and my family, and they expected Him to be true to His Word – that He would bring good and glory from terrible destruction. They did not force or manipulate me to stay the course and fight the battle, nor did they let me give up when I was exhausted and depleted.

They helped carry my burden while they continued to love, pray, and speak the biblical truth to me.

In life, and especially during times of struggle or battle, we need each other. One of the greatest tools the enemy uses against us is solitude and shame. If Satan can isolate us, he can trap us in darkness and obstruct the source of light which subsequently diminishes our ability to perceive reality clearly. Without Jesus Christ, the origin of light and truth, our path will not be properly illuminated nor can we be healed fully. Though we need authentic, intimate people to walk alongside us and share the weight of our burdens, there is no substitute for a sincere relationship with the Healer of our souls. On the battlefield of daily living, there will be times when you and I must walk a distance alone to commune with our Abba Father to seek and find rest, peace, hope, and healing.

God loves us so much and knows exactly what we need to become more like Him. He knew from the beginning that I needed the tragedy of my husband's addiction to break me, especially of pride, and to mold, shape, and hone me into the woman He intended me to be. Had I not walked this path, I would have never known the faithfulness and sovereign intimacy that the Lord of all creation has for me – one woman out of all humanity. The people He placed in my life to share the journey were purposeful as well. I have learned and gleaned from their committed walk with the Lord.

God is faithful, and we must not give up hope in whatever circumstance we face. Romans 5:3-5 assures us that our suffering produces perseverance, character, and hope. His hope will not disappoint us. These verses have been my lifeline, and I have not given up in seeking a supernatural marital and family healing. God saw it fit to do just that for my family and marriage nineteen years after the "I do," and I am deeply grateful. Had He chosen not to miraculously transform me, my husband, and my family, I would still be running the marathon, and my foxhole buddies would continue to be residing next to me.

Questions for personal reflection or discussion:

Review the phrases from the poem at the start of this chapter, and then answer these questions with those characteristics in mind:

1. Do you have at least one foxhole buddy with whom to share the burdens and joys of life? If so, are you entirely honest in revealing your struggles with that person and know she or he will hold your truth in confidence?

2. Are you a foxhole buddy for another? If so, your job is to bear the burden and love in truth – not to fix their circumstances.

3. Do you have an intimate and personal relationship with Jesus Christ? If not, true hope and healing will never be found. If so, are you diligent to pursue authentic intimacy with Him?

4. If you have a personal relationship with Jesus Christ, can you believe in faith that all circumstances He permits in your life He already knows about and that they are intended to make you more like Him?

5. Will you cooperate with Him, despite pain and discomfort, to be broken and molded into the woman or man He intended you to be?

CHAPTER 5

JOY IN THE MOURNING: RETURNING TO JOY
BY LINDA GILL, MSN, MA, LPC

In my sixty years of life, I have come to recognize that grief comes with every important loss we encounter. I have also come to understand that the more important or precious the loss, the deeper and more profound the grief will be. My journey has been one marked by important losses, all of them different and very precious. It has been equally marked by the important and precious losses encountered by others. The journey has changed me forever, and ultimately has led me through the pain to my life's passion and work – becoming a grief counselor called by God to give birth to the "Joy in the Mourning"® Center for Life Losses." I want to share with you the story behind the ministry to which I have devoted my life until God says "enough" or takes me home.

As a very small child, I remember sitting under our dining room table one night crying because our tropical angel fish was dying. Another time a bird was killed by one of our cats. My only consolation came from a precious older next-door neighbor who brought a bouquet of climbing roses from her fence and helped me have a "funeral" for the bird. When I was older, another not-so-nice neighbor intentionally poisoned my favorite cat. I keenly remember the anger and utter helplessness I felt as I witnessed such senseless suffering in another living thing. When I was in second grade, a classmate told me about her parents' divorce. She was the only child I knew who had experienced divorce, and I felt her pain as she told me how much she missed her daddy. I learned from her that grief can be about losses other than death.

I knew very early in my life that I wanted to help people. My journey toward that goal began one Christmas when, as a four-year-old child, I remember receiving my first nurse uniform – a bibbed white apron with a red cross on the bib and a white cuffed cap bearing a black stripe on the cuff – and a "doctor kit." The uniform had been lovingly hand-sewn as a gift to me by the wonderful neighbor next door who was more like a grandmother than a neighbor. From this point on, most of the time my dolls (as well as my little sister and playmates) became my "patients." The playhouse that my father built for us in the back yard was more often a "hospital" than the house it was intended to be. We had a surgery suite in the bike "garage" behind the little house. When I was older, my father even allowed me to use one of his camera lighting tripods as a pole for intravenous fluid administration. It worked just fine with a peanut butter jar taped to it complete with plastic tubing from my dad's fish aquariums!

As a young girl, I recall reading the "Cherry Ames" and "Sue Barton" nurse stories with delight. I dreamed of wearing a white uniform and cap and of somehow changing the world by easing pain and suffering. After high school, I chose to attend one of the last hospital-based diploma nursing schools in the country, the Watts Hospital School of Nursing in Durham, North Carolina. It was "practical," much less expensive than going to college, and my family doctor said that the best nurses he had ever worked with came from there. As student nurses, we lived in a dormitory on the hospital campus, took our classes there, and worked daily in the hospital except on weekends. I was fascinated by what I was learning about disease processes – and also what I was learning about caring for each patient as a whole person, not as just a diseased liver or ruptured appendix.

Critical care nursing held a particular fascination for me, and after graduation in 1971, I became an intensive care nurse. I got married that summer, and my husband's career moved us frequently. Over the course of time, I lived in five different states. In each new place I found a job, and it always involved some kind of intensive care work. Though I loved what I did, the "fit" was never exactly right. I've described it as feeling like a "square peg" trying to fit into a "round hole." However, in every setting, I found that my work always involved crisis, grief, and loss. Somehow I was drawn to patients who were critically ill or dying, and their families. I felt their experiences of loss keenly. Over the course of time, their stories of loss became intertwined with my own.

Early in my career, while living in Michigan, the first story unfolded. I met a wonderful couple while working in ICU. The husband was my patient, and he was critically ill from complications following a heart valve replacement. The new valve had become infected, and there was no way to heal the infection because the valve was not living tissue. There was also no way to replace the infected valve with a different one because the infection would have to be eradicated before a new valve could be put in, and my patient could not live without a valve in place. I was drawn in an incredible way to him and his wife. They had been given the news that he would not have long to live. They were Christians, very authentic in their faith, and their faith inspired me. It was solid even when the things they prayed for did not happen as they had hoped.

All of us were praying for a miracle. My patient rallied for awhile. Even now I recall happily the day that he felt like eating a hamburger, and also the one in which he was able to move to a room, no longer in ICU, where I continued to visit him frequently. His condition worsened after Thanksgiving that year. He and his family were told that he probably would not survive until Christmas. The miracle we received in answer to our prayers was not that he lived, but rather that he lived meaningfully while he was dying. Another miracle was that he lived long enough to spend Christmas with his family in his hospital room. I was blessed to have been a part of the life of this family. It was a window into how love and faith work during crisis and dying, and it was one of the most touching and humbling experiences I have ever had.

Another significant episode in the Michigan ICU was a midnight interaction I had with a mother who stationed herself at the side of her three-year-old daughter. The child had somehow gotten out of the house and behind the family car as the mother was backing out of the driveway to go to the store. She had backed over the child, and the little girl was dying from crush injuries. I remember the mother's tear-stained face as she said bleakly, "God must not want me to have a little girl. I'm a terrible mother! He is punishing me for running over her." I recall feeling totally helpless, not knowing what to say to her or how to help her. All I could do was cry with her.

In the mid 1970s, we moved to Illinois where I had my first "taste" of neonatal intensive care. Neonatal intensive care, the care of critically ill and premature newborn babies, was a relatively new specialty, and from the moment I started learning about it, I was "hooked." I remember a couple who had tried multiple times vainly to have a child. Each pregnancy had resulted in a miscarriage or early stillbirth. Finally, a precious and very tiny little boy, barely one pound in weight, was born to them. He was extremely premature and precariously alive. His lungs were severely underdeveloped. Over several months, he struggled to survive, and a mechanical ventilator was necessary to give his body the oxygen it needed. Though he grew and gained weight, the months of having to be on the ventilator took their toll on his lungs. The lung damage was so severe that he was never able to come off the machine, and he ultimately died. Over the months of his short life, I grew very close to his parents, and I found myself again immersed in the process of loving and losing as we moved together through his life and death.

In that same hospital, a baby girl came into the world, resuscitated after having been born without a heartbeat. She was severely brain-damaged and was never able to breathe on her own. She had wonderful parents, but she could never go home with them because she could never come off the ventilator. At this time, home care for medically-fragile children was non-existent. The hospital cared for her until her death several years later. Her parents had to process the loss of what might have been in order to accept and adjust to what was. It was an ongoing sorrow for them because of losses that related not only to her medical fragility and brain damage, but also to the lost dreams of having her home and having the opportunity to simply be her parents.

In the late 70s, while living in Tennessee, I worked in a pediatric intensive care unit and began to learn what a difficult and different kind of grief it is for parents and grandparents when a formerly healthy child is suddenly in critical condition or dying, or when a medically fragile or chronically ill child's condition worsens. During this time, I was also experiencing losses of my own. Seven years of infertility finally culminated in a pregnancy, but the pregnancy ended almost immediately with a very early miscarriage. I was at home alone when the miscarriage occurred. I remember being on the floor with my arms around the toilet bowl, weeping into it, knowing that a nearly-microscopic baby was in there somewhere amid the blood clots, and not wanting to flush the toilet, while knowing I had to.

My husband and I went through infertility testing and discovered that the problem was with me. We were told I would probably never be able to have a baby. So we began the process of adoption. After waiting for over a year on a state adoption list, we learned about a baby that was going to be born and placed for private adoption. Things went well for three months. The baby was born – a little girl. The evening before we were to bring her home, her mother changed her mind about the adoption. For me it felt like having gone through a pregnancy and then experiencing the death of the baby two days after giving birth. I was devastated – and angry. I could not understand why God would allow us to come so close – and then not let us have her. I was angry with every pregnant woman I saw. I was angry every time I cared for an abused child or for a baby born addicted to drugs because of its mother's addiction. I couldn't understand why they could have babies, and I could not!

At this point, I decided to go back to school to get a bachelors' degree in nursing. If I couldn't be a mother, I believed I could do something meaningful with my career if I had a college degree. It was during this educational interlude that I took my first class in death and dying. Mortality and loss were discussed and examined in multiple ways. I read Elisabeth Kubler-Ross's foundational book, *On Death and Dying*. My class even visited a funeral home and talked in depth with the mortician there. I was intrigued by this mysterious and deep thing called mortality and how it intersected with life and death.

In the early 80s, after receiving my degree, to my joy and amazement I became pregnant and was able to carry the baby to term. During labor, complications resulted in an emergency Caesarean delivery. My son was born not breathing. The birth was silent and terrifying. I was fully awake during the delivery, and as they lifted him from my womb, I could see that his color was blue. He was whisked out of the room for resuscitation. I had worked with enough babies to know that everything about his future depended on how long he had been without oxygen and how long it would take for him to breathe. The resuscitative efforts were successful, and he lived, but he spent the next twenty-four hours under observation in the special care nursery. I now understood on a very personal level the experience of terror when a child's life is hanging in the balance. I also understood the anxiety that resulted from watchful waiting that would show us whether or not he had suffered any brain damage at birth. To my relief, his physical and mental development were normal. However, until he finally walked at fifteen months, I could not be sure that he was really going to be all right.

After my son's birth, I began to work at Duke University in the NICU. Two experiences there changed my life and the direction of my work forever. The first was the birth of a little baby boy named Jonathan. He was born with a severe birth defect that required immediate surgery to save his life, and he had to be on a ventilator for a very long time after the surgery. I fell in love with this little boy – and with his parents. It was through their experience, and my experience with them, that I learned how to truly help parents to be parental in an intensive care setting. There were many complications following Jonathan's surgery. The complications were unavoidable. All of them resulted from treatment necessary to save his life but that caused other problems over which we had no control. I now saw through the window of closeness that developed with his parents, a first-hand, long-term experience of the grief that comes from having a child who is much-loved but critically ill – and then chronically-disabled. To this day, I am still in touch with Jonathan's mother, and I eagerly follow the progress of his life through her Christmas letters.

The second life-altering experience was the short life of a tiny infant born with a heart malformation that could not be corrected and was incompatible with life. After multiple resuscitations, she finally died. I vividly remember going into the staff lounge, beating my fist on the wall, and saying angrily out loud to God, "Why do I stay in this insanity? This hurts too much!" I have never heard God speak to me audibly, but immediately after my question, I "heard" words in my mind that I knew were not my own thoughts. The words were, "You do it for their families."

At that moment it was as if a conception took place – the conception of a dream that would later become my life's work. I knew that I couldn't "fix" the pain of parents. I also knew that medical science wasn't powerful enough to always save or "fix" lives so that the outcomes were always good. I realized that it was the "magic" of walking with people through the most dreadful experiences of their lives that made the difference for them. I couldn't change their circumstances. I could not save or heal their children, but I had the power to change how they experienced these things. And I could bring with me the power of God's love and compassion. The burning desire of my heart was to make a difference in the lives of as many families as I had the opportunity to touch.

In the meantime, in my own life, another life event had occurred. My father had a stroke. It caused complete paralysis of his right arm and partial paralysis of his right leg. My mother cared for him at home for the remaining years of his life. I watched her live out her love and commitment to him, and I also watched how her faith in God sustained her and gave her strength. For the last few years of my father's life, I was fortunate to live close enough to my parents that I was able to go home frequently to help my mother care for him. I vividly remember the Christmas before Daddy died. He was having trouble breathing, and he had lost a significant amount of weight. He and I spent Christmas Eve together in the emergency room. He was dehydrated and received intravenous fluids, after which I was allowed to take him back home. During this time, he and I had the most meaningful and important conversation we had ever had – about his wishes when the time came for him to die. One wish was to be at home and not in the hospital when he died.

He shared that he did not want to be kept alive by machines or artificially fed in any way. He also told me that he had made his peace with God – finally having settled some questions he had struggled with over the years concerning the deity of Jesus Christ – and then he shared with me his assurance that he would go to heaven after he died. As we discussed these things, he was fully lucid and seemed to be entirely at peace.

After that conversation with my father, my mother, sister, and I all agreed that we would abide by Daddy's wishes to the extent possible. I tried to get his doctor to order hospice care for him, but he said he couldn't be certain that my father's condition was terminal. He said he couldn't order hospice care unless he could be sure Daddy would die within six months! I could *look* at him and tell that he was dying! I told the doctor that, if he would support us as *we* provided hospice care for Daddy, if he would not pressure us to put him in the hospital, and if he would come to the house to pronounce him dead, we would continue to allow him to be Daddy's physician. However, I also told him if he could not promise that support, we would change doctors. He was able to agree to this.

My father died quietly on February 13, 1985, not quite two months after our conversation in the emergency room. He never had to go to the hospital again, and he was never fed artificially. My mother remained his primary caregiver, with me and my sister visiting as we could on the weekends to help her. He went into a coma one morning and died just after 4:00 PM that afternoon. I was en route, trying to get home to be with him. About fifteen minutes out, I felt impressed to pray that God would allow Daddy to die peacefully and not let him have to suffer a long time. When I arrived at my parents' home, I was met at the door by a deacon from their church who told me that Daddy had died just a few minutes earlier. What a comfort it was to me to realize that I had been praying for him at the moment he died, and that God had taken him home within that single day and without suffering.

At the time of my father's death, my son was a month shy of his third birthday. We did not take him to the funeral, but I did tell him that Grandpa had been sick for a very long time, and that he had died. The night of the funeral, as I was tucking him into bed, he asked, "Mommy, what's 'died'?" I had always been told that, when a child is big enough to ask a question, he is big enough to receive an honest answer on a level he can understand. I tried to think of a way to explain death to such a small person. The story I told him, and the little game I played with him to help him understand that dying is not the same as sleeping, seemed to satisfy him.

It was not until he was ten years old that I realized how important the story had been for him. One night he repeated to me the story I had told him so many years before and asked lots of questions about his grandfather. I realized then that the story needed to be published to help other children. In 2005, the little book *"Mommy, What's 'Died'?" The Butterfly Story* was published with my son as its illustrator. Since its publication, it has been used in public schools, in hospices, and in funeral homes. More recently I have adapted the story to help grieving children in third world countries. It has been used successfully in several different countries by International Christian Hospice in the incredible work they do to train church volunteers to help those who are dying, and their families.

After my father died, another devastating loss in my personal life was the death of my marriage and subsequent divorce four years later. During the separation, I moved to my hometown to live with my mother, and returned to school to get a master's degree in nursing, specializing in parent-infant nursing and focusing specifically on crisis and grief intervention with families of critically ill or dying infants and children. I remember being told by one of my professors, "You will never get a job as a nurse doing that."

Undaunted by her discouraging words, I graduated in 1989 and went to work in the NICU at Baptist Hospital in Winston-Salem, North Carolina. I loved the work I did with families. I learned how to provide support for families whose babies were dying – and how to include them in everything that was happening along the way. I remember specifically being with the parents of a six-month-old baby boy who had such severe lung damage that he could no longer get enough oxygen, even with the ventilator. They were given the option of taking the breathing machine off and allowing him to die. After they had received this news, they asked me to come into the room with just the two of them. I remember that we sat in silence for a while. It was a heart-wrenching time for all three of us.

The mother finally asked me, "Linda, if he were your baby, what would you do?" I breathed a prayer, and I was given words again in my head that went something like this: "We have technology that can prolong life and often save it. But the same technology that can prolong life can also prolong suffering when the outcome is not going to be life. You have done absolutely everything as parents that you can do to give your son every chance at life. So have the doctors and everyone who has cared for him over the months. I think he is telling us that he can't do it anymore and that he is too tired to keep fighting. I think he is dying, and that no matter what we do, we can't keep that from happening. I also believe that he is suffering because of the lack of oxygen. To take the breathing machine off would allow him not to have to fight anymore. He could just be a little baby, without tubes for the first time, and allowed just to be held in the warmth of your love as he slips away. That would have to bring him so much comfort – to be held while he dies rather than dying in a bed hooked up to all these machines and intravenous tubes."

They chose to remove the machines. His daddy held him while we took away all the tubes. He then carried him to a family room where he and his wife – and other family members – had the opportunity to be together, holding him, kissing him, and loving him from this life into the next. He lived for several hours. It was precious and meaningful time for them – and for me. I was in the room only to check on them at intervals and to check the baby's heartbeat and breathing. He appeared to be comfortable and not suffering. They were suffering, but there was a peace that did pass understanding in that room, and there was something comforting to them in just being able to care for him during those moments at the end of his life. Several months later I received a card from his mother recalling how meaningful the experiences of both his life and his death had been to them.

In 1991, I moved to Columbia, South Carolina – a casualty of a corporate "downsizing and reorganization." I went to work again in NICU. About six weeks after the move, I realized that the work I was doing was not a good "fit" for me – again the "square" peg trying to fit into a "round" hole. I turned in my resignation and immediately started looking for other work while working out my three-month probationary commitment. I decided that, if I couldn't find something in my specialty area of grief and crisis, I could work comfortably in pediatric home health care. I interviewed at another local hospital. There were no clinical specialist positions open at that time, but I was told that budget preparations were underway for the next fiscal year, and if approval came for the position, I would certainly be their choice for working with new parents as a clinical specialist/educator on the maternity unit. I thought it sounded like it could really be fun, especially after all of the stresses and losses of the previous six years.

I discovered soon that God had a very specific plan for me and that, as I was experiencing all the "bumps," crises, and losses in my own life, He had been laying out a plan that only He could have engineered. The week after my last day at the previous hospital, I received a phone call offering me a job in the newborn nursery at the hospital that was considering me for the clinical specialist position. I was asked to meet with my new supervisor after my first day of orientation so that we could "write the proposal" for the position they were hoping to secure. When I met with her, I asked, "So, we are going to write a proposal for my working with new parents, right?" She said, "No – remember all those 'unusual interests' of yours in your resume (grief, loss, crisis)? We have decided we want you to do all those things, as well as educational programs for parents. What do you think?"

What did I think? I think it was a miracle straight from the hand of God! The proposal was approved, and that October I started my new role as the clinical nurse specialist for perinatal family care in the area of the hospital that cared for women and children. It soon expanded to crises with infants and children in the emergency room as well. God used this experience to show me two things. First, He can do anything He wants to do (even when "nobody will ever hire you to do that" as my former professor said). He has a plan and purpose, and He will do it. Second, I learned that this work was the most rewarding, amazing, exhausting, and satisfying work I had ever done. I now knew beyond a shadow of a doubt that God had called me to it and had prepared me for it. It was a perfect fit for this "square peg!" I had finally found the right hole!

And – as a special gift, God also gave me a new husband. Several years earlier, Jim had experienced the death of his wife Sandra following a battle with breast cancer. From the beginning of our marriage, he has shared my dreams, encouraged my vision, and supported my work.

I worked at the hospital for five years, at which time there was another corporate restructuring. My job was eliminated, not because it wasn't valued, but because it didn't provide revenue. (I discovered that insurance doesn't pay to help families through crisis, grief, and loss.) Though this was disappointing, God had shown Himself so faithful during other hard times that I knew I could trust that He would continue to lead me.

He used an "anonymous donor" to give money to the hospital foundation, specifically to be used for "bereavement care." I was asked to become a self-employed clinical nurse specialist working under a contract with the hospital to continue to provide services to families who experienced critical situations and deaths related to their children. My current work Joy in the Mourning® was the result. Psalm 30:5 says that "Weeping endureth for the night, but joy cometh in the morning" (KJV). My husband wept when I told him the name that God had given me for this work. He said, "That's true: You cry through the long night of grief, but if you do good mourning, you come back to your joy."

Since 1996, when Joy in the Mourning® started, I have been back to school – this time at Columbia International University, earning a master's degree in clinical counseling. I wanted to be able to do more for people who experience all kinds of life losses than

I could as a nurse. I am now a licensed professional counselor who specializes in losses of any kind. As my own life experiences have taught me, there are many kinds of losses other than death. The most exciting part of my work is that God has moved it into another chapter. Joy in the Mourning® Center for Life Losses was founded in 2002 and is a developing non-profit organization. Our mission is to provide programs and people to help individuals and families return to the joy of living after any kind of life loss. I am so excited to be a part of what God wants to accomplish through this ministry.

As I write, I reflect on the past two years. During that time, my mother died from dementia, and I experienced the "empty nest"– two more significant losses. My life has been a wild ride, and it isn't over yet. However, every experience, no matter how painful and difficult, has been used by God in my personal life and in the work I am doing. I wouldn't trade a minute of it, and I would be willing to go through all of it again to have learned the lessons He has taught me and to be doing the work I am doing. I serve an amazing God! To Him be all the glory!

Questions for personal reflection and/or discussion:

1. Linda's vision of a life of helping others started very early, when as a child she imagined herself a nurse, and then developed the characteristics to match the calling. When you were a child, what did you imagine yourself doing as an adult, and to what degree have you been able to fulfill that vision?

2. While nursing, Linda was drawn toward helping those in extremely difficult situations. What characteristics does it take to function well in that kind of setting? Describe people who have helped you in difficult times.

3. Linda's story involves multiple losses, including infertility and

an adoption that was called off at the last moment. How might you have (or how have you) responded in similar situations?

4. Review the chapter with a view toward identifying and listing all the losses Linda describes. (In a group setting, have someone compile these for the group.) If there are other kinds of losses not mentioned in the chapter, that you or others in your group have faced, add them to this list, then share briefly what happened, and how they have affected you over time.

5. Linda has experienced a renewal of hope and fulfillment of her dreams to establish a ministry to help others because God specializes in reversals, using our weaknesses to help us become strong in Him, and comforting us in all our troubles so that we can comfort others in any distress with the comfort we, ourselves, have received (see 2 Cor. 1:3-4). How have you seen this truth express itself in your own experience?

CHAPTER 6
NARRATIVES FOR LIFE
BY PEGGY HARTSHORN, PHD

As a child I was fascinated by all the old things (loosely called "antiques") in our home, mostly given to us by elderly family members to fill the gigantic old home on East Main Street, in Lancaster, Ohio, that my parents purchased in the early 1950s. This house was home to our family – three little girls, I the oldest, my mother and father, my little brother who was born seven years later, and also to my father's new podiatry practice. My parents had chosen Lancaster, an ideal small town in many ways, to raise their family and "hang out the doctor's shingle" because it was geographically half way between my two sets of grandparents in northern and southern Ohio.

To fill the many large rooms of that old house, mother and her three little girls went regularly to auctions on Saturdays at old farm houses, sometimes even buying "mystery boxes," with one item on top that mother wanted, but odds and ends underneath that we little girls cleaned and marveled at when the box came home. But our favorite place to browse and shop was in the barns, basements, and attics of elderly relatives. We would often come home with a rickety rocking chair, cut glass vases, knickknacks, or old family pictures in ornate frames. (A far cry from favorite home furnishing stores today like Target and The Great Indoors!)

I live with many of these dear family items today, an "accident of history" perhaps, but I think rather a part of God's providence because they keep alive for me the great role models He provided, that I now know have had a profound impact on my story. I was always surrounded by a "great cloud of witnesses" (Hebrews 12:1).

On my desk as I write is a beautiful portrait of my Great Aunt Ladora (Aunt Do), once a missionary nurse. She was my mother's aunt. As a child, I remember her as a tiny, gray-haired maiden lady (less than five feet tall) who wore cotton house dresses and black tied oxfords with chunky heels, and who made mysterious pitchers of fruit punch with real orange slices floating on the top. But even then I imagined her as she was in this familiar picture, taken in 1937: In her late 30s, her hair long, dark, and braided, in full native Sioux clothing made of white leather with long fringes, and red, yellow, green, and brown beading in swirling designs on the bodice, arms, and scalloped edges. On the bottom she had written, "U.S. Indian Nurse, Apache, and Oklahoma." When the framed picture came into my possession, many years later, I was shocked to find that she did not wear that costume daily in her missionary work, as I had romantically imagined; her handwriting on the back indicated, "My dear mother wanted me to have my picture made in Indian costume. I went to the pawn shop and borrowed this costume!"

Aunt Do's suitor had died in the influenza epidemic of 1918, so she studied nursing in Chicago and heroically devoted the rest of her life to the service of the Lord through serving others. I saw that firsthand as she cared for her ailing mother and then her sister in their home until they died. She never ceased reading her Bible daily, nor did her faithful, joyful spirit ever wane, even as my mother and I prayed with her at her bedside and sang her favorite Methodist hymns as she died peacefully at age 103.

In fact, I had "saints" and humble servants of the Lord on both my mother's Protestant side of the family, and also on my father's Catholic side. When I visited my father's mother in Portsmouth, we walked through the alley in early morning darkness to daily Mass in candle-lit St. Mary's church. In her Victorian home, I studied pictures of relatives like my grandfather's sister and his niece, Sister Aquin and Sister Thomas Aquin. They were both dressed in flowing black habits, with large crosses around their necks and pure white wimples surrounding their faces. They gave up traditional family life to make Christ their spouse. Two older cousins on this side of my family became priests and one became a nun while I was growing up.

The desire to follow in the footsteps of these "ideal" family heroes, who sacrificed all to be used by the Lord, grew within me as a child.

So did the expectation that I would marry a wonderful husband and have a large family. I believed that children were a blessing. Some of my playmates in Lancaster were from families of twelve, fourteen, even sixteen children, and sometimes I felt sad that I did not have more brothers and sisters. I simply expected that I would have many children, and an ideal marriage, like my parents. They were crazy about each other, and my dad would often tease my mother and give her pinches and kisses as she made dinner in the kitchen.

I didn't realize at the time what a gift it was to have my father home almost all of the time, since our home was also his office. Between patients he came into our living room and sat in his special chair, where his favorite reading materials were books about our faith. He was always available to help with homework, answer tough questions and, in his gentle but sure way, set us straight about God's truth. My mother was a nurse, but after my father's practice was established, she no longer took special duty nursing jobs. My sisters and I walked home from school every day for her home made lunches, and we often woke her up from a short nap when we got home in the afternoon, then helped her with cooking, cleaning, sewing, and her many household projects.

I loved school and my teachers, worked very hard and did well, and took leadership roles in my class and extracurricular activities. Both of my parents were involved in our church, school, and community. Prayer was a major part of our day: morning, mealtimes, every time a siren was heard on Main Street, and before bed. I felt very close to Jesus. We never missed church on Sundays, even on family vacations.

When I share about my childhood, people often marvel. One of my friends says I grew up in "Happyville." I was not concerned about exactly how the Lord would use me in that world, I was just taking life one step at a time, working hard at the tasks given, feeling secure and loved by the Lord and by all around me. To me, my life was normal. The world as I knew it was a beautiful and orderly place.

The real world occasionally intruded, but not enough to disillusion me. In 1960, when I was a seventh grader, my grandparents took me to visit my great uncle Carl in a small town in Arkansas. There was only one black (then called Negro) family in Lancaster, viewed as quite "upstanding." The father was a long-time employee of the country club, and his son was elected president of his class at Lancaster High School. The Civil Rights Movement was unknown to me. In Arkansas I saw, for the first time, "shanties" on stilts with extended black families sitting in front of them, gazing at us as we passed in our car. I loved visiting my three older Arkansas cousins at their impressive, marble-halled, high school. I didn't even think about the fact that it was all white. Two years later, I was shocked and saddened to learn that their gorgeous school had burned down. It was not until I was in my 40s that my cousin, with whom I had lost contact until then, said, "Didn't you know? After court-ordered integration, the men of the town decided that having no school was better than having an integrated one, so they burned our high school down." How could I have been so ignorant?

In 1964, the major shock of my childhood was the assassination of John F. Kennedy, our young and glamorous President with the ideal family, a beautiful wife, and two charming children, confirming in his public image what American thought itself to be. When the news of events in Dallas was broadcast, our principal's voice came over the high school loudspeaker, we all rose, and she led us in prayer. Like the rest of the country, my family could do almost nothing but stare at the TV screen as the events of the next few days unfolded before our eyes, including the shooting of Lee Harvey Oswald while under police custody. Camelot was surely ended, but what that really meant was still unclear.

I went to a traditional women's, Catholic, liberal arts college in an idyllic community near San Francisco from 1965-69, where I had outstanding, faith-filled men and women as teachers and mentors. Mike, my tall, handsome, red-headed high school sweetheart (whom I had known since first grade), was in college back in Ohio. Every other day he wrote a love letter to me, and I responded. We talked on the public pay phones in our dormitories perhaps twice a month, keeping the calls short because every minute was so costly. We saw each other at Christmas and during the summers, very romantic times. All was well in my personal life and on my serene campus.

However, only fifteen miles away, buildings at Berkeley were being burned down by anti-Viet Nam war protestors, and in San Francisco the hippie movement was being born. My friends and I visited Haight-Ashbury, intrigued by the strange sights and smells, thinking this phenomenon an odd tourist attraction.

The reality of what was happening in the "sexual revolution" was not yet evident. But it was becoming clear that all was not well in the world. During my college years, Martin Luther King, Jr., and Bobby Kennedy were also assassinated. California became one of the first states to decriminalize abortion, and billboards advertising abortion began to appear. Our ethics professor warned us, "Mark my words. Abortion will be legal all over the United States in five years." That was 1968. I still remember that a quiet gasp rose up from the girls in the class when he made that terrible prophesy. Somehow I imagined that my sense of the world going "topsy turvy" was limited to the world in California. Subconsciously, I must have believed that once I got back to Ohio, all would be made right.

I was engaged to Mike in my senior year of college, and we were married in June of 1969, very soon after our graduations, in a seemingly perfect ceremony, surrounded by the church and our happy families. We were both starting graduate studies at The Ohio State University. The next few years flew by in a blur. In our first year of marriage, my father, aged forty-seven, suffered greatly from esophageal and stomach cancer. In his dying weeks, he wanted to be able to see from his bed our picture of Jesus as depicted in St. Luke's gospel (22:42), kneeling and praying in the Garden of Gethsemane, "Not my will but thine be done." My mother, coming home from church one day during that terrible time, shared her conviction that the reading was a sign that Dad, such a wonderful man, would have a miraculous cure. The reading was Psalm 92:12: "The just shall flourish like the palm tree" (NAB). My father, always the leader of our family in faith, pointed to the suffering Jesus in the garden and said, "Honey, there is the just man." His heroic battle, yet constant trust in the Lord and His divine will, left us knowing that he taught our family how to live and also how to die.

Meanwhile, Mike and I, suffering in our relationship, had come to realize that our expectations about marriage were entirely different but equally unrealistic. He had come to marriage from a broken family where the conflict had been painful (his parents separated when he was six), and he expected that we would never disagree. I expected the ever romantic, easy "give and take" that characterized my parents' relationship. Hurts and misunderstandings were common and not resolved. I decided that we had taken vows for life and that marriage was "for better or for worse." Ours happened to be "for worse." We would resign ourselves to that state. Later, we learned that a name for the life we had settled for was "married singles."

Amidst our married single lives, where we each pursued our degrees, then careers and separate friendships, we had some moments of marital intimacy and good times, just enough to convince us that we had a relationship we both could at least tolerate. We had been married several years, and I was not yet pregnant. Since I was still pursuing my PhD, I was just as happy, but began to suspect that we had an infertility problem. My expectation of the perfect marriage and large family was disappearing. "Happyville" was a distant memory. I felt distant from the Lord, absorbed in the stresses of our lives, trying to keep an "even keel" using my own strength, willpower, and resources. The character trait that God would someday use in His service had not yet been surrendered to Him. I was still in charge of my life.

But my life was changed forever by what happened on January 22, 1973. I was driving in my car down High Street near Ohio State (where I was in the final stages of getting my PhD) when I heard on the radio that the Supreme Court had just ruled, in their decision called Roe v. Wade, that all laws restricting abortion in any way in the United States were unconstitutional. That terrible prophesy from my ethics professor, "Mark my words . . . ." rushed into my mind. It had been almost exactly five years. Mike had just started law practice, so as soon as I could reach him, I said, "You have to go to the law library and research this decision – surely it can't be true!" But it was. It seemed to me that this decision was in opposition to everything America stood for – starting with the "inalienable right to life" and protection of the weak and powerless. Therefore, it was a threat to our way of life.

It was also in opposition to the core truths of the Christian faith – that we are all made in the image and likeness of God, and that we are so valuable to Him that God sent His only Son Jesus, who died for our sins so we could have eternal life. Therefore, it was an affront to God. Up to that point, there had been no contradiction for me between the core values of our country and my faith. Our country was fast becoming a place I could not relate to, whose values I could not accept. I realized that I had been wrapped up in my own little world for the last five years, focusing inward, not paying attention. This was my brutal wake-up call.

I knew I had to "do something." Little did I know that the Lord would use this moment as the first step toward a wonderful adventure of stepping out in faith that Mike and I have been on since, deepening our relationship with each other and with the Lord, and, for me, giving me a purpose and mission in my life and allowing me to be used by the Lord, as I had always prayed as a child. But I am getting ahead of my story!

I had heard of an organization called Right to Life (I don't remember exactly how). As soon as I finished my dissertation, I looked them up in the phone book and called. Ed, the president, told me later that he only came into the office for about one hour per week, to sort the mail and make lists for volunteers. When I called, he happened to be there. I no longer believe in coincidences. They are better called "God-incidences"! When I told him I wanted to "do something" and "be useful," he invited Mike and me to his home to learn more about abortion. His wife, Meade, was a pediatrician at Children's Hospital and he was an economist. They had gotten involved a few years earlier because pro-abortion groups (Planned Parenthood, National Abortion Rights Action League, National Organization for Women, and Religious Coalition for Abortion Rights – all of which are still active today) had been campaigning to change our laws state by state, so Right to Life had been formed.

Ed and Meade showed us a slide presentation, first with beautiful pictures of developing babies, then with pictures of aborted babies. I had seen one picture of an aborted baby previous to this, on the cover of what I believe to be the first pro-life brochure, "Life or Death," published in Cincinnati, Ohio. Now I saw many pictures of aborted babies from about eight weeks to twenty-four weeks of gestation. I think I was somewhat in shock, but I was highly motivated to do whatever I was asked to do, which turned out to be speaking engagements and debates in schools, colleges, public forums, radio, and television. Ed and Meade were wise mentors. At a group meeting in about 1975, there was a question about whether we could get a Human Life Amendment (to overturn the Supreme Court decision) in five years, or would it take us ten? Ed turned to me and said, "We have to learn to be long distance runners, not sprinters." That was over thirty years ago, and we are still running the race.

Even though I was now an English professor at a local university, I became more and more involved in pro-life work. People were calling the Right to Life office not only for information, but also to get help for people considering abortion. The first abortion clinic in Columbus had opened, competing with the chartered flights that took place on Saturdays to a New York abortion clinic, all arranged, sadly, by the local Religious Coalition for Abortion Rights. Ed and Meade were housing a pregnant girl, and, when another girl needed housing, they asked Mike and me if we would take her in. We said "yes" immediately and opened our home to Anne, the first of twelve girls that the Lord sent to us over a period of about ten years, six of whom made adoption plans and six of whom became single parents.

I was still not pregnant, but I felt almost like I carried and birthed a baby because I experienced pregnancy at almost every stage with Anne. I helped her through Lamaze classes, was her labor coach, and assisted in the birth of her son, Michael. My husband Mike and I were there as Anne made her adoption plan, and we were also present with the adoptive couple when Michael was welcomed into their family and church through baptism. We could not have imagined that twenty-five years later we would be present when Anne met and hugged Michael again, for the first time since he was three days old. A few days later Michael married Tara, also adopted. Both birth mothers were present at the wedding and were honored by their children and the adoptive families! Wow, what a day!

While housing Anne, Mike and I discovered that we had the kind of infertility problem that could not even be treated. Our only choices were the relatively new "artificial" reproductive techniques, which our church teaches are not ethical, and adoption. At first I could not believe that the diagnosis was hopeless. I went to the library to do some research on my own. In the car on my way home, after verifying the truth, the reality hit me. I had to pull over, sobbing for several minutes.

Then, almost in a flash, a great sense of peace came over me. It was the peace that St. Paul talks about (Philippians 4:4-7), the "peace that surpasses all understanding." When I arrived home and discussed it with Mike, I told him I knew that parenting was an act of selfless giving to build God's kingdom, but perhaps, since we could not have our own biological children, God was calling us to give the gift of ourselves in some other life of service to Him. Mike, however, felt strongly that we should adopt. I was very willing. We knew, from our pro-life work, that abortion numbers had been increasing very quickly since 1973. At the same time, the number of infants available for adoption was dwindling proportionately.

Cultural values were rapidly reversing, and they would continue to do so for the next thirty years. When I was growing up, even outside of "Happyville," most children were born into a two parent family, divorce was not common, and sexual relationships outside of marriage were socially frowned upon. If pregnancy occurred, either adoption or marriage was the choice. Homosexual relationships were rare. Abortion was only legal for "therapeutic" reasons, such as to save the life of the mother.

Societal norms changed dramatically after 1973, all part of the agenda of Planned Parenthood and its allies. It was only evident in hindsight that they had orchestrated the rapid advance of the sexual revolution through changes in American law. A change in birth control laws in the 1960s established the so-called "right to privacy." Sexual mores changed rapidly as birth control became common. The

Roe v. Wade decision in 1973 was based on reading the new "right to privacy" into the Constitution. An unfettered right to abortion was needed to guarantee that babies could be eliminated as the embarrassing and complicating result of recreational sexual activity.

I believe that God's perfect plan for our sexuality was announced in Genesis with the creation of Adam and Eve, made in His image (with all that means about their relationship to each other and to Him) and with His command to them to increase and multiply and fill the earth. This plan – God Himself, self-giving love, marriage between a man and a woman, sexual intimacy, and children all go together – was intentionally taken apart, and our culture has been left with the misery and suffering that results: misery such as escalating rates of not only abortion, but also of fatherlessness, divorce, domestic violence and child abuse, drug and alcohol abuse to mask the misery, high rates of infertility due to sexually transmitted diseases, post abortion trauma, and broken relationships with God.

The good news is, however, that the church, the Body of Christ, has been raised up and activated, especially in the pro-life movement, and we are beginning to see not only individual healing and reconciliation, but also reversals in these trends and destructive cultural markers!

None of this I knew, of course, back in the mid 1970s. All I knew was that I was becoming more and more passionate about my pro-life work. God was using me, and Mike and I wanted to adopt and have a family. In 1976 we adopted Timothy Michael, and in 1979, Kathleen Margaret – both miracle stories, but I will only tell you Katy's! After we adopted our precious little baby Tim, I was still teaching full-time at the university and working every spare moment for the "cause." We were busy and had no idea we would soon be "stopped in our tracks" and re-routed, so to speak.

Mike and I made a Marriage Encounter weekend in October of 1978. On that weekend we had a dramatic re-awakening of our faith and our personal relationship with the Lord, and we committed ourselves to giving up our "married singles" lifestyle and becoming a sacramental couple – that is, allowing the love of our marriage to be reflected outward as a sign of Christ's presence in the world. As St.

Paul's letter to the Ephesians tells us (5: 21-33), husbands and wives are called to love each other as Christ loves the church, giving up their lives for each other, as Christ gave His for us. That sacrificial love for each other (and by extension for our children) was our call as a couple. We agreed that our "coupleness" could be reflected through making our pro-life work a "couple ministry" – we would together start a pregnancy help center in Columbus.

God showed me on that weekend that I had neglected Mike and our relationship for our new baby, my pro-life speaking circuit, and my career. I decided to resign from the university. When I made the announcement to our faculty body, the feminists (and many others) told me I was wasting my education; they were upset and unsupportive. Don, an accounting professor and fellow faculty member, came to me later and told me that he knew my decision was from the Lord. He and his wife had begun praying for me, and the Lord had told his wife that we would be sent a baby girl. That was in early 1979. That April, on Palm Sunday, the week before Easter, we received a totally unexpected phone call. A little girl had been born, and her mother was just then making an adoption plan. Would we be interested in adopting her? Palm Sunday is the day my father died, and we knew that this baby was another "God-send," just for us from Him.

Our two beautiful children are now married and we have four grandchildren. We could not be happier with our wonderful family. While our children were still babies, and through most of their teenage years, Mike and I were on the leadership team of Marriage Encounter, giving talks and weekends, sharing the details of our relationship and our struggles as we worked to truly be a sacramental couple. I believe this experience wove us, with the Lord, into such a strong cord, that we have been able to withstand tremendous challenges, pressures, and attacks. We have grown in our love for each other and for the Lord, and we have now been married for over forty years. We still meet monthly with two other former "team couples" to challenge each other in our relationships and to remind each other that "love is a decision," and it can only come from the grace of God, the source of all love.

The couple ministry we committed to on that original Marriage Encounter weekend in 1978 became Pregnancy Distress Center (now called Pregnancy Decision Health Centers) that we opened on January 22, 1981. The 24-hour hotline was installed in our bedroom three months before the opening, so that our number would be in the new phone book published in January. We had no idea that the phone would begin ringing immediately with people wanting abortion information and pregnancy help. The information operators were giving our number even before the phone book was published! We were housing pregnant girls, fielding phone calls, plus caring for our children, about two and five years old at that time. Soon I was volunteering as a peer counselor in the office (and several branch offices that were opened in the next few years), answering 24-hour hotline calls, and helping pregnant women, especially those vulnerable to abortion, both inside the offices and out. After the Lord, Mike, and our children, pregnancy help (and advancing the pregnancy help movement) became the passion of my life.

Our house painter once asked if he could bring his girlfriend over one evening to talk to me. Becka was adamant that she had to have an abortion. She had reared, almost single-handedly and while working several jobs, two beautiful twin girls who were now ready for college. She could not jeopardize their future by having a baby. Adoption was out – she could never give her baby away to strangers. She said she was praying and reading her Bible daily, and she was sure God would forgive her. Just then our Katy, now a young teenager, came home. I asked her if she would mind coming into the living room, meeting Becka, and sharing how she felt about being adopted. Katy, generally quite shy, shared beautifully and openly about the love and gratitude she had for her birth mother and her choice for life, and she shared how happy she was in her adopted family. I knew the Holy Spirit was inspiring her because her words were perfect, although she did not know Becka's story. We all shared a good cry. Becka decided not to have an abortion. Unfortunately, she lost her baby in a terrible car accident, in which she also almost died. She felt God saved her partly because of her choice for life, and she later became one of our hotline workers.

A few years ago, Tim also shared with me how he felt about being adopted when he told me that he was sure God had a purpose for his life. He shocked me when he said, "I feel God saved my life once when I was not aborted, and then a second time when you and Dad adopted me." Although we do not know if his birth mother ever even considered abortion, he feels like many of his generation born after 1973 – they know they are "survivors." Many, like Tim, feel that God must have a purpose for their lives. Others, who know (or suspect) that they have siblings who were aborted, feel like the "wanted" child. Sometimes this puts tremendous pressure on them; they believe that something they say or do can make them "unwanted." The pressure can become too much for them. Abortion survivors need to know that at least one person, the Lord, loves them unconditionally.

This is only one of the effects of abortion. There are so many others. When I started in the pro-life movement, I knew that abortion kills babies. I soon met the first of many women (and men) whose lives had been shattered by abortion – physically, emotionally, and/or spiritually. I met still others who had been left with the physical scars of sexually transmitted diseases (some of which can never be cured) and the emotional scars of sexual trauma from premature sexual relationships and multiple sexual partners. These are the walking wounded. I could tell you so many heart-breaking stories. I came to realize that abortion does far more than kill babies – it takes us on a downward spiral that is destroying women and men, families, and our culture.

In response to the women (and men) the Lord presented to us, our pregnancy help center pioneered programs not only for crisis intervention, but also for post abortion recovery and abstinence until marriage education. Our abstinence program was funded by a "Model Program Grant" from the U.S. Department of Health and Human Services (HHS), under President Reagan, and I was asked to serve on an advisory board (and grant reading panels) for HHS in Washington, D.C. Later, we were one of the first centers in the country to add ultrasound medical services and provide a "window to the womb." I followed the Lord, one step at a time, for twenty-two years, leading our pregnancy help center first as director, then as chairperson of the board. Mike, despite being a busy attorney, supported me every step of the way. He handled all our legal work, even the depositions for a frightening law suit filed against the HHS Model Program Grant recipients, including our pregnancy help center. The case went all the way to the U.S. Supreme Court. Their landmark decision established that a faith-based organization can receive federal funds, as long as these funds are not used to "proselytize," and it made possible the faith-based initiatives of recent memory. When you say "yes" to the Lord, He takes you on quite an adventure!

In my years of pregnancy help center leadership, volunteer counseling, and couple ministry, at no time did I believe that I was working out of my own strength, knowledge, power, or wisdom. I was always in situations where I had no expertise to rely on! I am a perfect example of the saying that "God does not call the equipped; He equips the called." I knew the Lord was teaching me through the experiences He was giving me, primarily teaching me what it means to step out in faith and trust in Him.

The greatest reward I have received from surrendering to Him is a deeper love for God – as He shows Himself to me daily in the fruit that He brings from my meager, though heartfelt, efforts. The second greatest reward is the joy I experience working with Christians from all faith expressions – Catholic, Evangelical, Mainline Protestant, Charismatic, Apostolic, Non-Denominational, Orthodox, and others, who have all been called into our movement. They contribute to this great work, which we sometimes call "Cross Bearing for the Child Bearing," with their time, talent, and treasure. I believe the Lord is using our movement of brotherly love to help bring His church together, around the world, so that eventually we can all be one, as Jesus prayed on the night before He died for our sins.

For the past sixteen years, I have been President of Heartbeat International, formerly called Alternatives to Abortion International, the first network of pregnancy help centers, maternity homes, and adoption agencies founded in the United States in 1971. It is the "umbrella organization" that our pregnancy center joined when we were incorporated in 1980, and whose board I joined in 1986. Heartbeat is now the most expansive pregnancy help network in the world, with over 1,100 affiliates in forty-eight countries. Heartbeat is the leadership training pipeline for the pregnancy help movement. We also operate a 24/7 contact center that drives over 250,000 calls, e-mails, and instant messages each year to centers in the USA and Canada. And we have a special outreach to our international affiliates and to cities where abortion clinics outnumber pregnancy help centers (sometimes over thirty to one). We are specially mentoring the African American and Hispanic leaders in our midst, because their communities are targeted for abortion. We defend and protect centers from attack, both on a state and national basis, primarily through a pro-active message that "pregnancy centers are good for America." Representing Heartbeat, I have had the opportunity to share my experiences and what the Lord has taught me, to pregnancy help center leaders on every inhabited continent.

The Heartbeat network saves about 2,000 babies per week, and serves approximately one million people per year, and we are funded almost entirely with private, charitable dollars. Twenty-nine out of thirty people working in our centers are volunteers, making us one of the greatest volunteer movements in American history, and perhaps even in the history of Christ's church. Soon our pregnancy center in Columbus will be celebrating its 30th anniversary, and Heartbeat International will be celebrating its 40th.

We are also making great progress in returning our country to its root values, in helping restore those who have been wounded in the years since Roe v. Wade, and in winning hearts and souls for Christ. For the first time since the question was first asked, the Gallup poll reports that over 50 percent of Americans describe themselves as pro-life, and only 36 percent describe themselves as pro-choice. Abortion rates and teen pregnancy rates are dropping. Programs such as the post abortion recovery and the abstinence program started by our pregnancy center so many years ago, plus many new ones, are being used successfully all over the USA, and translated into many languages around the world. Heroic men and women are now speaking up publicly, saying, "I regret my abortion." Even the Supreme Court, in a recent decision upholding the ban on partial birth abortion (a type of abortion done in the second and third trimester by partially birthing the baby, then killing him or her before full delivery), stated that many women suffer deeply from their decision to abort.

But so much more needs to be done. Abortion continues, and many people suffer its "secret shame," believing Satan's lie that they have committed the unforgivable sin. As Ed taught me many years ago: we are not sprinters, we are long distance runners (as St. Paul describes himself in his second letter to Timothy, 4:7). I have realized recently that this is also a relay race. I need to prepare to pass the baton. Just as the Lord has led me as I stepped out in faith through the years, I know He will lead me in the "hand off" and help me finish strong, whenever the time is right.

The little girl from "Happyville" who wanted to be used has been given a wonderful opportunity to be of service, but the greatest reward is that God has shown Himself to me in so many ways, and I have learned to know and to love Him more and more. It seems almost as a bonus that He has also given me the desire of my heart in a wonderful husband and beautiful children and grandchildren. People sometimes tell me that they believe I will eventually know all the children whose lives have been saved through the work of pregnancy help centers – someday when we all meet in heaven. Then I'll even have that really big family I know God has in store for me!

Questions for personal reflection and/or discussion:

1. When she was still just a girl, the author often prayed, "Lord, use me." If you have ever prayed a similar prayer, how has that prayer been answered? If in a group setting, describe the process through which you were prepared and then have been used by God to advance His work.

2. "Happyville" was a fictitious name for the entire context in which the author grew up – her friends, her family, her community. All were so good and positive. Is there a word that describes the

context in which you grew up? If studying alone, write down the first word that comes to mind. In a group setting, share that word and describe why you think it came to mind.

3. Do you think that it's easier for someone to get personally involved with a cause such as the pro-life movement if all they ever knew was "Happyville" and all that goes with it?

4. On the other hand, do you think it is necessary to have encountered significant adversity in order to embrace a calling from the Lord to support or participate in a cause that is aligned with the principles of His Word?

5. What cause or causes have you been involved with, and what were the short-term and long-term results (in helping fulfill the group's purpose, or within yourself). If you've not been involved with a cause thus far, with what causes would you like to become involved?

CHAPTER 7

SHANNON, GONE TOO SOON
by Suzanne Foster, MA, LMFT

December 20, 1991, began like any other morning, except that I had been looking forward to it for a number of weeks. It had been a very tough year, and my kids and I had been hit from all sides by a number of difficult circumstances – a health scare, financial difficulties, job loss and an eventual change of employers, health issues with my children, and a myriad of other issues that seemed to pile one on top of the other with no relief in between. It had been a difficult few months on my job as a sales representative for a fundraising company, and I was exhausted. I was looking forward to two weeks off and spending Christmas with my daughter, Shannon, and my son, Steve.

Shannon had just returned home from her sophomore year at UCLA and was going to start a part-time job that day. Steve was a freshman in high school and was just starting his Christmas break. After Shannon finished work, we had planned on going Christmas shopping and then going to our favorite Christmas store at Horton Plaza in San Diego to purchase their special ornaments – something we did every year. It was a family tradition, one that I started when they were babies. As they got older, they enjoyed choosing their own ornaments and usually selected one that meant something special to them that year. The idea behind this was to give them their own box of ornaments for when they got married and started their own families.

I checked on both of my children before I went downstairs to start my morning routine. Both were sleeping, but I noticed that Shannon was breathing very heavily, and I thought that she might be getting sick. I made a mental note to check on this and make a doctor's appointment if necessary. I knew she had had a tough fall at college with her full load of classes and her part-time job. She was finding college more difficult than she thought it would be and wasn't pleased with her grades. She had been an honor student in high school and was disappointed that she wasn't pulling straight A's at UCLA. Because I knew she was tired and might be sick, I decided to let her sleep a while longer before she had to get up to go to work.

When she wasn't up by 8:00 AM, I was concerned and went in to wake her up. I called to her several times, and when she didn't move, I went into her room. It was then that I noticed that she wasn't breathing. I started to panic. She was lying in her bed; her body was warm. She had a smile on her face, but her coloring was all wrong. I yelled for my son to come, and then I called 911. Steve came into her room to see why I was yelling. He saw his sister and knew something was terribly wrong. The lady who answered the 911 call asked us to get her on the floor and to try CPR. She then asked if there was a pulse, which there wasn't. She then said to me, "She's dead."

I was in shock. "What do you mean she's dead? She can't be dead." My poor son didn't know what to do. He took the phone from me and talked to the operator. She told him she was sending over the police and coroner. In a fog, I made several phone calls to my pastor, Shannon's father, and a close friend.

Within minutes the police were in my home asking me questions. I didn't know what had happened. She went to bed the night before and was dead the next morning. I realized that they needed to question me because they didn't know the cause of death – until one of the policemen found an empty bottle of prescription pain pills in her room and several open bottles of over-the-counter medications. She had ingested enough of everything to kill her. Suicide? Not my daughter. That wasn't possible. There had to be some mistake.

The coroner came and took her away, and I didn't get to say goodbye. My baby, my first born, gone without a goodbye.

Shannon's father and his wife came, as did my pastor. Somehow people were notified, and for the rest of the day people were in and out of my home. A big part of me wanted to be alone just to process what had happened, but I wasn't left alone at all. My son was devastated. He had lost a step-sister to a brain tumor a year before, and now his own sister was gone. I was concerned for him because of his own battle with depression. I was afraid that I might lose another child. However, I didn't know how I was going to help him when I didn't know how I was going to help myself.

Somehow we got through her funeral and memorial service. Thankfully, her father made the arrangements for the funeral, which was ok with me. I was not in any condition to do that. My job was to plan her memorial service. I'm a doer and planner and just knew if I kept busy planning the service, I would be OK. Her memorial service was beautiful, and the church was filled with family and friends. Several people shared what Shannon had meant to them.

We got through Christmas, but it was very difficult. On Christmas Day my son went to stay with his father, and I was alone for the first time in five days. Never having lost anyone close to me before, I didn't really know anything about grief. I remember thinking as I took down the tree (which we never did finish decorating) that I would probably be over this in two to three months, and life would go on. I figured that if I read some books and maybe talked to a counselor, I would get through this OK. After Christmas, I called a Christian ministry, Focus on the Family,* and got the name of a therapist. I also read everything I could get my hands on about grief and suicide, which at that time wasn't a lot. I felt somewhat prepared for the grief journey which was to follow.

However, I was not at all prepared for the depth of emotion that followed Shannon's death. But, no one ever really is prepared when it's a sudden death, and especially when it's a suicide. I went over and over in my mind what would cause a beautiful and intelligent young lady to do such a horrible and final thing to herself. I asked "why" a thousand times, really believing that if I had answers, it would help me feel better. Was it something I had done? Her father? Her boyfriend? What could it have been? I know my last conversation with her the night before she died was very difficult, and I felt such guilt about that. I just knew that conversation had pushed her over the edge. As time went on and we did find out more about some of the things she had been going through, it became evident that it wasn't one single event, but a combination of things that had made her life seem overwhelming and hopeless.

I went through every emotion possible – from sadness to anger, denial to guilt, and I felt the most intense pain I have ever known. At times I really thought I was going crazy. I thought about her every waking moment, and she inhabited my dreams. There was no rest from this nightmare. People told me just to take it one day at a time. For me, in the beginning, it was more like one second at a time. And the memories – everything reminded me of her and sent me spiraling back in the abyss of pain. I didn't know how I could survive such horribleness.

I did start therapy, and even though the therapist had never dealt with a suicide, it was wonderful having someone to talk to and be real with my feelings. I had quickly discovered that most people, even those close to me and who knew her well, were uncomfortable talking about the manner of her death. Some refused to even consider that it was a suicide. Indeed, the coroner did rule it an "accidental" death, but in my mind it was a suicide. I believe she intended to end her pain and despair in the only way she felt she could at that time. Suicide is very difficult for people to talk about. It is the "elephant in the room," and I found that it was best just not to talk about it because people were uncomfortable. Therefore, having a paid professional to talk to was very healing and a real blessing. It is necessary for survivors to talk, and talk some more, but many won't because they don't feel safe with others. This is why it is important to be in a support group or other setting with people who have been on the same journey, so you can share your story with fellow pilgrims.

Somehow I managed to go back to work after Christmas, though it was very difficult. It was all I thought about, and there was nothing to divert my attention. I worked and lived alone most of the time except for every other month when my son was with me. All I really wanted to do was to go to bed and not get up. For several months that's what I did on the weekends – I would go to bed on Friday night and only get up to eat and let the dog out until I had to get up to go to work on Monday. My grief was complicated by depression, which I didn't know much about. It took a wise therapist to diagnose this several months after Shannon's death and to prescribe medication.

Shannon had been depressed also, and I hadn't recognized it because I didn't recognize my own. I have since learned that approximately two thirds of people who complete a suicide are depressed. Most depression is undiagnosed and untreated. Depression left untreated leads to hopelessness and despair. I know this contributed to her decision that December night. It also helped answer some of the "why" questions that plagued me.

I walked through the first four months in a fog and then hit my own low spot of hopelessness and despair. This was especially true when the shock and numbness wore off, and I hit the "wall" of reality. I realized I wouldn't see my daughter again in this life and didn't think I could live five, ten, or even fifteen years without seeing her. I was in such despair that I wanted to end my own life. Thankfully, through some interventions that I can only attribute to God, I was able to get through that time.

I had read that grief was linear and that there were five stages of grief. I found out that this is not true. Grief is really more circular, and I found myself going through some of the same emotions over and over. The sadness would subside somewhat, and then something or someone would remind me of her, and the pain would return. Guilt was something that was deeply felt and long lasting. After all, I must have been the worst mother in the world for my child to end her life. All of the more "ugly mother" moments kept replaying over and over in my mind, and I just knew that had I not said or done such and such, she would not have felt so hopeless. I now realize that all parents have "ugly parent" moments and that this, by itself, is not the reason why children choose suicide.

I remember on the second anniversary of her birthday after her death when the guilt and sadness were just eating me alive. I had an appointment with my therapist. He asked me why I felt so guilty. I told him because I had been the worst mother in the world. He asked me if I thought she was in heaven with Jesus. I said I had peace that she was. He then said the most profound thing to me that has helped me over and over through the years: "Why are you beating yourself up? She doesn't see you that way. She sees you as God does, perfect through the blood of Jesus." I have shared this with other parents who are despairing after a suicide, and it has brought them comfort.

God intervened in big ways during my darkest times. I started a grief class four months after she died and that was a lifeline for me, as was a survivor of suicide support group. I continued in counseling, which was helpful, especially after my depression was diagnosed and treated. During this time, I went to Arizona to visit some friends. They saw the despair I was feeling and suggested I talk to a former pastor of theirs who had written a book on grief. I talked to Bob Dietz for two hours and felt so much more hopeful after that conversation. He assured me that I was right where I was supposed to be in the process, especially considering that I was in mid-life and all that entails.

Anniversary dates were very difficult, especially that first year. Mother's Day was probably one of my more difficult days. I still struggle with Mother's Day. Every "special" day evoked memories of her and of happier times. I learned to plan ahead for those days and not let them broadside me. I usually made plans with a friend to do something special. On her birthday and death day, I always made plans to go to the cemetery with a friend and then have lunch or do something else enjoyable. I felt by doing this I was remembering my daughter, but taking care of myself at the same time. I recommend this to others who are grieving a major loss, especially if the loss is a suicide.

Gradually, as time passed, it did get easier. Though I don't believe time heals all wounds, time passing does make them "softer" and less painful. I found myself able to go for longer periods of time without thinking about her. I was finally able to take care of her things, and invited her friends to take something of hers that they wanted. I was able to visit with her friends and to enjoy talking with them about her. The sadness came when I had to say goodbye because I knew that I probably wouldn't be seeing several of them again. Her best friend from high school has kept in touch, and I've been able to celebrate her marriage and the birth of her own children. I couldn't have done this in the beginning, but it's been wonderful having that connection to my daughter through her friend all these years.

Suffering through a traumatic loss such as a suicide changes most people's perspective, and this was certainly true for me. I just didn't look at life as I had before Shannon's death. Little things that had bothered me before she died became not so important any more. Her death helped me to get my priorities straight. It became more about relationships than about my job and other activities. I realized that life is so short, and some people are gone before we have the chance to tell them how we feel about them – how much we appreciate and love them. I remember telling those who came to my house in the early aftermath of her death to go home and love their families and not to put off telling them how they felt about them. My perspective became more about having a purpose, and I knew that whatever I did with the years I had left on this earth, it had to have purpose and meaning.

Because grieving is different for every person, there is no time table. At the one year mark, several people remarked that they couldn't believe I was still grieving, as if I should have been "over it" by then. This was difficult to deal with. Grieving a suicide can be very lonely because it's difficult to find people who still want to talk about the loss, or want the individual to talk about it, especially when it has been several months since the event occurred. It was understandable that people went on with their lives, but my life had stopped and hadn't really gotten started again. There were a few close friends who were wonderful and caring during this time. One friend sent a funny card every week for several months. Another friend called every afternoon and told me a funny joke and inquired about my dog. I had told him that if I ever lost my sense of humor and gave my dog away, he needed to worry. His, "just checking" was very important to me.

I knew when it was time to move on. I was finding joy in everyday activities again and in renewed relationships, and was ready to do something different with my life. I had been in a job for eleven years that just wasn't fulfilling any longer. I knew I wanted to help others who had lost loved ones to suicide and who had had other major losses, but I wasn't quite sure what that would look like. I had in my heart to write a book and to lead workshops on grief, and suicide grief in particular. I made the decision to go to graduate school and get a Master's Degree in counseling as I felt the MA behind my name would help open doors and windows of opportunity for me to do what I believe that God had placed on my heart to do. It was time to find my "new normal."

Two years after my daughter's death, I headed off to graduate school. I knew this was exactly where I was supposed to be and that God was going to use this in His plan for my life. As I worked towards my Master's in Marriage and Family Therapy, I found graduate school to be very challenging and rewarding. I learned a lot about myself and about people in general. I ended up going on for my Doctorate in Psychology, but life intervened, and I wasn't able to finish it. I had several exciting internships where I was able to put my education and training into practice. As I worked with hurting people, I was convinced that I had followed the right course for my life and that all my pain and suffering were going to be used to help others heal.

While in graduate school and afterwards, I volunteered my time with a wonderful organization in San Diego, Survivors of Suicide Loss, as a support group facilitator. I was also on the speakers bureau and had the opportunity to speak to high school and college students about suicide prevention and what it is like being a survivor. Hearing a survivor's point of view had a big impact on those students, because they never really realized what it was like for those left behind. For many of them, suicide had seemed an option when life got really tough. I hoped that by sharing my story, many lives were saved.

In 2003, I received an e-mail from Dave Biebel, a friend who lived then in Colorado. Dave and I had lost touch for several years, so I was surprised to hear from him. Dave had just completed a book for Zondervan Publishing Company on depression. They asked him to submit a proposal for a book for survivors of suicide, and that's why he contacted me. He remembered about Shannon and thought I could help him with the proposal. I was excited to be involved – it was time to tell my story and to do something proactive to help other survivors.

It was a long and difficult process, but our book, *Finding Your Way After the Suicide of Someone You Love*, was published in June of 2005. It was very rewarding to see something in print that we hoped and prayed would help others. The opportunity to write this book was a gift from God to me, and I feel very blessed to have been a part of it.

Survivors of suicide need help and support from those around them. They have so many immediate needs in the days after the suicide and as they travel their grief journey. They need to talk and tell their story, so it's important to have supportive people who are willing to listen. It's also important for people to be there for them in the weeks and months after the loss – to accept them for what they are going through and not condemn them for their grief or the manner of the death. Survivors cannot heal alone – they need a caring community.

While living in San Diego, I was working for the County of San Diego as a social worker for Child Protective Services. This was a position I held for seven years. It was a very rewarding, but stressful job. Before the book was published, I felt that God was calling me to leave my job and to move to Nashville, Tennessee, to be a part of the ministry of Music for the Soul. I had never lived anywhere but in California, so to leave everything and everyone I knew and move 2,000 miles to an unknown setting was a daunting prospect, to say the least. It was also very exciting to think I could be a part of something that I was so passionate about. So, in June, 2005, I made the move across the country to see what God had in store for me.

Since being in Tennessee, I have gotten involved with the Tennessee Suicide Prevention Network and work in the area of survivor support. I have also developed a faith-based curriculum which follows the outline of our book. I lead support groups for survivors who want to talk about their loss and their issues of faith.

Leading these groups has been very rewarding, and I know I've grown as a result.

I don't know all that God has for my future, but I do know that He has redeemed my past. He has truly made beauty from ashes. In the immediate aftermath of Shannon's death, I couldn't imagine how something so horrible and so painful could be turned into something that would bring healing and comfort to others. When I went to graduate school hoping to eventually write a book and to speak to hurting people through conferences and workshops, little did I know that God was going to use my pain to fulfill the dream He had placed in my heart. I'm very grateful that my story has helped others who are reeling from the pain of losing a loved one to suicide.

Questions for personal reflection and/or discussion:

1. What were you feeling as you read this story? Choose one word, and then, in a group setting, share that word. Have someone record all the words that are shared.

2. Did reading this story help you understand your own loss, even if it was not related to suicide, in a new way?

3. If you have ever experienced the death of a friend or family member through suicide, tell that story briefly, and also share the relative difficulty you've experienced in trying to support those left behind.

4. Many people experience a "crisis of faith" after a severe loss. If this was true for you, describe the feelings and how you resolved them.

5. What Scripture, hymn, or inspirational poem best helps you in the recovery and moving on phase?

* Information on how to reach Focus on the Family is available in the Appendix related to Organizations.

CHAPTER 8
AND HE WILL GIVE YOU REST
BY LISA COPEN

I remember as a teenager reading the book *Joni* by Joni Eareckson Tada, and being impressed with the amount of strength she revealed by sharing not only the things she was able to overcome, but by revealing how weak and vulnerable she felt becoming a quadriplegic at the age of 17. Up until that point, I had been exposed to your typical church or ministry that was founded on simply a call God had given an individual. By reading Joni's story, I saw firsthand how a much-needed ministry was rooted in the experience of one who had gone through a fire of refinement accompanied by personal suffering, rather than one who had gone to seminary to follow a calling. It was a memory that would stick with me.

Years later, as a college student, I debated about what area of social work I should go into. I volunteered at organizations such as the Rape Crisis Network and a hidden home for battered women. Although I could take an unlimited amount of classes and volunteer many hours, I had not experienced what these women had gone through. Of course, I was extremely grateful to the Lord that He had not sent me down these particulars paths of "education" so that I would be qualified to offer my personal experience; however, I found it difficult to connect on a level that I wished for, in order to offer my best.

After four years of college and hundreds of hours of volunteer work, I was simply burned out and still without a degree. I went to my parents and confided, "I can drop out, or I can flunk out, but I have to take a break." Fortunately, they were extremely understanding and trusted my judgment that the break was necessary. I worked in a retail establishment selling clothes and was extremely relieved that if I sold a woman a scarf that was not her best color, her life was not at risk because of my advice.

I followed my heart from Oregon to San Diego after falling in love with a man who wrote amazing love letters and talked to me for hours on the telephone. He would become my husband five years later. But at the time, I was driving up and down the coastline, wondering what God's plans were for my life, and singing the worship song, "He who began a good work in me will be faithful to complete it," with tears streaming down my cheeks. God provided places to live and jobs, but oftentimes it was at the last minute that He would come through. I had decided counseling was not my calling and that I would rather work for a nonprofit with a cause. So when I was hired to work at a large nonprofit corporation, I was eager to work my way up through the organization to a position of working with their programs, fund development, or the membership department.

My job description was to fill in for whoever was unable to come to work that day. I was the lowest person on the totem pole, and I was expected to be in two places at a time, covering for practically every job position for a variety of services. This included working in a little store, rolling tents, writing thank you letters to donors, doing bulk mail of thousands of pieces of mail, being the receptionist, and anything else my supervisor thought I should be doing at that time. In reality, it was a frustrating job where I was the pawn between managers who all fought for a level of control, so I could not please everyone. A few years later, I would come to appreciate the experiences I had there, however, and be grateful for the wide range of skills I'd been taught that were instrumental in beginning my own nonprofit organization. It was one of those moments when you know that God has always been in control, even when He was working "undercover."

One morning I awoke at the age of twenty-four with a wrist that seemed to be frozen into place. The thought of simply moving it was too painful. I was not alarmed. I had been lifting boxes and rolling tents the day before and assumed that it was just an average sprain. My supervisor was concerned because she had secretaries who had been having carpal tunnel surgery, so she took me off all computers so I could heal quickly. I assured her that I thought it would heal in a few days, and life would return to normal.

That was the last time I was able to define the word "normal" in the typical fashion of most people. Within days, although my wrist began to heal, the other wrist froze up, and then it went from shoulder to shoulder, elbow to elbow, knee to knee, hip to hip. After numerous visits to see my general practitioner, who was unsure of what could be causing these flares, which were accompanied by extreme pain, I went to see a doctor of internal medicine. She spent over an hour asking me what seemed to be a series of unrelated questions and then did lab work. Within twenty-four hours she called me with a diagnosis: rheumatoid arthritis.

This was in 1993, when Internet access was just starting to become available. There was not yet an online environment where I could look for in-depth information about what my future might hold. When the doctor called me with the diagnosis, I bluntly asked her, "On a scale of one to ten, ten being normal, what will my life be like?" She tried not to answer with a specific number, but I told her I needed to know what to expect and what kind of battle I was up against. She reluctantly said, "If you're lucky, maybe six."

I hung up the phone with mixed emotions. Although I was relieved to have a name for this pain I was experiencing, I did not understand the term "chronic illness" or "autoimmune disease." Up until that time, I had been quite sheltered from any form of chronic illness in my circle of relationships. I had the mindset that illness was something that happened to people when they got "old." I had the ignorant assumption that anyone who was perfectly healthy at the age of twenty-four should simply be able to take a few pills for ten days and then recover.

In the coming months, I would go through a roller coaster of physical pain as a physician tried to find the medication that would best work for my condition. I would sit down on the floor to watch a movie and, two hours later, not be able to stand up. One morning, I had to call my supervisor at work at 7:30 AM, and tell her that I literally could not open my own door because my hands and wrists were too swollen to both grasp the knob and turn it. Ironically, the week of my diagnosis I had purchased my first new car that had a stick shift. I would grab the stick with both hands while steering with my knee, and shift while I screamed to get into the next gear and my shoulder back "into place."

I continued to work for another nine months as I waited to get in to see a rheumatologist with the goal of finding an effective treatment plan that would work with my body. At the time, the newest medical action was to put someone who was recently diagnosed on "all the medications" available for this disease, and then gradually wean her off of them as she went into remission. Unfortunately, all of the medications they put me on I had to stay on and eventually increase the dosage to have the treatment be effective. In the seventeen years I have had rheumatoid arthritis, I have not yet experienced any level of remission, only degeneration.

I resigned from my job and went back to college to finish my BA in sociology before my disease became disabling. I wanted to complete my degree so that my career goals would still be a possibility. The year that I graduated, I also married my sweetheart, who stood before our family and friends and pledged that he would love me in sickness and in health. He has never left my side, and his commitment to me and our son, and his dedication to providing for us is the reason that I am able to follow my passions.

My husband worked about seventy-five hours a week to support us until I finished school. As I started to go on interviews, they would go well until the interview was complete, and then my knees would lock up and I would be unable to stand, or I would not be able to open the door as I left. I saw my career dreams quickly fading away. Though God graciously took care of us, leading my husband to a job that financially provided (literally, in the week we were to run out of money), I began to grieve the loss of my dreams and my identity that was ingrained in them.

So, as I went into the deepest emotional and physical valley of my illness, simply trying to get dressed before noon and to complete at least one household chore before my husband came home, I asked God, "What now?" We had planned to start a family, and were trying to decide if we should immediately apply to adopt a baby or try to conceive first. Though reluctant, my doctors assured me that, if I wanted to be a mom, I should try to accomplish that sooner rather than later – to not wait to "get better" because it likely would not happen. After a year of trying to conceive and my health failing, I went back on all of my medication, and we started the adoption journey.

Not wanting to get caught up in the depressing state of putting life on hold indefinitely while we waited for a baby, I remember telling the Lord, "I need something . . . I don't want to get obsessed with the pursuit of a child and miss the plans you may have for me while I am waiting." I went to the library and checked out stacks of books on how to start a nonprofit, how to write for magazines, how to self-publish your own books, and more.

I spent a few years volunteering for the Arthritis Foundation. It is an amazing organization, and I found a great deal of comfort through understanding my disease better. However, I found that there was no place to be able to express my faith in Jesus, as well as my spiritual struggles. I was trying to understand how one can completely believe that God will heal, yet at the same time, wonder if healing is truly God's will at that time.

I helped write their monthly newsletter, but I became weary at simply offering people the advice to have one more cup of hot tea or a bubble bath to make all of their pain go away. In my experience, the only thing that was going to get me through a life living with chronic disease was to cling to Jesus, and to know that God had a purpose in the pain. I believed my pain would never be wasted, and that though I would struggle with how my life could be defined by this illness, I was still living in God's "Plan A" and not in God's "Plan B." This was the hope I wanted to offer people, but I was restricted in what I could write for this secular organization.

I sought out Christian support for people who lived with chronic illness and was unable to find a support group or ministry specifically outreaching to people with chronic illness. I had assumed there was at least one main organization for people who lived with illness, but I could not find it.

I remember going to the Christian bookstore after my first appointment with the rheumatologist, and the only books on the shelf in my area of interest were how to "die with dignity" or how to survive cancer. "Where are the books for people who live with chronic illness?" I asked a store clerk. She said she couldn't think of any and went to ask other clerks. She came back and said that was quite an interesting idea; there were a number of people who she knew who had illnesses such as diabetes and arthritis who would find a Christian resource rather helpful.

Based on the lack of Christian resources for those with chronic illness, I could have easily assumed that I was the only one who had not yet been healed, despite my faith. Thankfully, I knew that my pastor had rheumatoid arthritis, and he was one of the first people I went to for advice and encouragement for this unexpected detour in life. I remember him praying with me and asking God to heal me, while lightly grasping my hands with his own hands that had started to show deformities.

I recalled the impact that Joni Eareckson Tada had on me years earlier, and I had the opportunity to go and hear her speak. My husband and I stood in a long line of people waiting for her autograph afterwards in order to have thirty seconds of her time to ask her if she knew of specific Christian ministries for people who lived with chronic illness. I was beginning to think that this was what God had called me to, and I was feeling an indescribable peace because I felt like God had answered my desire to be able to experience the actual path of suffering that those I encouraged were on. If there were such a ministry, I wanted to be a part of it. If there was not, was this where God was leading me?

Joni was very supportive when I told her of my desire to start a chronic illness ministry and said she was not aware of any ministries I would duplicate. She expressed how great the need was and basically told me to "go for it!" I never looked back or questioned how God would create a ministry where there was limited energy and no budget.

On the one-year anniversary of my husband's new job, he received his first bonus and purchased our first computer with it so I could be connected with the world. He was working long hours at his regular job during the week, then working Friday and Saturday nights doing gigs with bands, and then playing at church on Sunday morning. He was doing everything he could to support us financially while also eager to see where God would lead my growing interest in chronic illness ministry.

I logged on to the Internet from home and immediately saw great potential in being able to reach out to others who live with chronic illness and also connect them with one another. Before my illness I had had a great deal of energy and was spontaneous and social. I missed people. Between my illness and my husband working many hours, the Internet became a wonderful connection outside of my apartment. There was a large patient community growing on the Internet back in 1996, as those who lived with different health conditions sought out information on their own in order to become better advocates for their health care.

In my own church, people had expressed an interest in getting together and talking about their faith and illness and being a support to each other. However, because of the variety of illnesses, schedules, and transportation issues, getting together had become a bigger challenge than we had expected.

My best attempt to bring us together was through a small newsletter that I began called "… And He Will Give You Rest" based on the Scripture, "Come to me, all you who are weary and burdened, and I will give you rest" (Matthew 11:28). Soon thereafter it was going across the country as people shared it. With extremely limited computer knowledge, I built a small website and posted articles about chronic illness and faith. On the website I mentioned this monthly newsletter and asked for a $15 donation to help me cover photocopying and postage expenses. Surprisingly, people actually began to send me checks in the mail. In 1997 Rest Ministries, Inc. was born.

Subscribers to the newsletter wanted to know who else was receiving it so they could connect with one another on the Internet. "Share and Prayer" was our first online group. Next came our first support group in our community called "HopeKeepers." Some drove from over thirty miles away, often accompanied by their spouse, and whatever it took to make them comfortable for ninety minutes. We met at the local library with people packing in large pillows to sit on, small pillows to hold up an arm or support a knee, bottles of water, Bibles, and more. Since there were not any Bible studies about chronic illness, I wrote a five-lesson study called "When Chronic Illness Enters Your Life," and we used this to guide us through our mixed emotions while keeping the focus on Christ and not just on our aches.

God took over from there and expanded the ministry in ways I never could have imagined. Over 300 HopeKeepers groups are currently active, our newsletter has turned into a magazine, I have self-published a number of books that have financially supported the ministry for years, and my Internet provider called to see what I was doing that brought 80,000 visitors a month to our website. We have published daily devotionals for over ten years that one can receive each morning via e-mail. And the ministry has been featured on national television and radio programs.

I have had the joy of being able to experience my passions, writing and speaking – all in the context of sharing God's love for those who are hurting due to illness. In 2004, I had a "full circle moment" when Joni and Friends ministry called to see if I would be interested in being an affiliate of their organization, specifically for those with illnesses or invisible disabilities. It's been a joy and an honor to now be a part of Joni's ministry.

In order to reach out to the many people who live with chronic conditions who do not know Christ, we began National Invisible Chronic Illness Awareness Week in 2002. It has grown to become a full virtual conference with twenty speakers giving seminars in a five-day time period over the Internet where one can "attend" for free and without ever leaving the comfort of home. Our annual conference has become a well-recognized and respected event by the online patient community, and we've reached hundreds of thousands who would not have previously visited our Christian website.

So, how exactly does someone who lives with daily pain and a degenerative chronic illness actually run a national ministry? I could not tell you a formula except that I take one day at a time. Rest Ministries' website looks like we are a large organization with staff members and an office. Our office is my home office, and I wear many hats. I have one assistant who is a volunteer who helps me return phone calls and answer e-mails. She lives in Oklahoma, and I have, in fact, never met her in person.

The only reason that we have been able to continue to grow and reach so many people is mostly due to the fact that people who discover Rest Ministries find encouragement for themselves, but then they immediately turn around and encourage others. We have a large social network called the Sunroom. Here, one can connect with about 1,600 people and find those who have similar illnesses, or those who are in related situations in life such as homeschooling, parenting, marriage, etc., while also living with a chronic disease. We aim to be one of the places where God will set the lonely among family (Psalm 68:6).

While we do have writers who may have credentials attached to their names such as "reverend" or "doctor," the person nearly always lives with a chronic condition. Those who read the daily devotionals from Rest Ministries or articles on our website will find that they are written from the perspective of someone who is still currently living with a chronic illness, not by a healthy person who was trained to teach people with illness how to live. Sometimes, the actual event or spiritual struggle shared in a devotional or article may have occurred within the last forty-eight hours.

It is this level of authenticity from our volunteers that makes Rest Ministries both a comforting and a safe place. Everyone admits they struggle, while clinging to the promise that God will never abandon them. There is no substitute or slick marketing campaign that can replace the willingness of people to allow their weaknesses to be seen in order that God and His faithfulness can shine through. I remember reading about how we are like wet sand near the ocean. If one were to poke a stick into the sand over and over and make holes, like the problems in our life can feel, each hole is immediately filled up with the ocean's water, which can be compared to God's love and presence. No matter how many holes are in our lives, God can immediately fill them if we allow Him to.

Sharing one's vulnerabilities and Christ's strength is one of our greatest assets. The Bible says, "That is why, for Christ's sake, I delight in weaknesses, in insults, in hardships, in persecutions, in difficulties. For when I am weak, then I am strong" (2 Corinthians 12:10, NIV). We can read this and say, "Yes, I believe that to be true." But it is human nature in us to want to appear like we have it together and to not reveal our weaknesses, lest we be judged.

Following my joint replacement surgery in four fingers on my left hand, I became brave enough to take down my glossy professional photo of myself and replace it in my newsletter with a snapshot of me a few days after surgery. My hair was straight, my face was puffy and full from prednisone, I had not showered in a couple of days, and I had a cast on my hand that was over eighteen inches around. I found it interesting that I received e-mails from people who said how grateful they were that I had revealed my "true self" and how much more they could relate with me after seeing the snapshots of me post-surgery than they could with my professional photo.

Another time I poured out my heart on a blog post about just being tired with the daily-ness of living with a chronic illness. One woman e-mailed me and said, "After three years of receiving your newsletter, today you became real to me. I will pray for you."

The greatest strength of ministries that are born from suffering is that the people who are involved have walked the walk and are sharing their time and story simply out of compassion, in order to make another person's journey slightly less lonely. Doctors, counselors, pastors, chaplains, and others in the professional helping fields have experiences that can help them facilitate a person through a difficult time. However, I believe that we should never rule out people who have or are "walking the walk" simply because they do not have a title linked to their name. One of the few requirements of our HopeKeepers group is that one of the people in the leadership role must actually have an illness. He or she can have helpers, and we encourage them to do so, but nothing takes the place of someone who has been through a similar challenge.

Telling our story is important. Every person has a story that is unique. If you take ten people diagnosed with the same chronic illness on the same day, at the same age, their experiences will still differ. And that is one of the reasons that God has given each person his or her own testimony. Regardless of what people may say about your beliefs, they cannot take away your testimony.

There is a great deal of controversy regarding the theology of healing. Many people still believe that the only reason a person has illness in his or her life is due to sin. When a person with a chronic illness shares his testimony of how God has used the thorn of an illness to His glory, it's not uncommon for listeners to want to step in and tell him how he has the power to change the outcome of his testimony by following whatever formula they think is necessary to receive God's healing.

Some people have been told that their "testimony is wrong," because God never wants His people to suffer with illness. Many feel that their testimonies are not good enough because in the end they are not sharing how God healed them physically – but rather how He has healed them spiritually.

As the director of Rest Ministries, I have received my share of e-mails telling me I am doing a disservice to the Lord by allowing people to see how God can be glorified in one's life despite the existence of an illness. I believe that God can heal and that He still does heal people every day in our world. But I do not believe that there is a specific formula that a person can follow and be guaranteed a healing.

Our testimony is one of the greatest gifts God gives us, and Rest Ministries has become a safe place where people can share their testimonies along with the fears and challenges that accompany an illness. They can share without fear that they will be judged or placated with simple theology such as, "Just give it to God and it will all be fine."

Nearly one in two people in the United States lives with some kind of chronic condition such as diabetes, heart disease, fibromyalgia, or multiple sclerosis. Many people also live with constant chronic pain from conditions like migraines or back pain from car accidents. Most of this pain is invisible, and the person who is suffering may hear the words, "But you don't look sick," or, "But you look fine."

I often encounter churches that are reluctant to embrace the chronically ill community because there is an unspoken assumption that the church will be weighed down by their needs as well as depressed by the fact that these people are not healed. After all, if church is supposed to be an example to the community on how wonderful life can be if one walks alongside Jesus, what message would be sent if it appeared that some members had given up on the hope of being healed? What are we communicating to our visitors about God's healing power if there is an announcement in the bulletin about a chronic illness group meeting? Won't those people with illness always need something like rides, meals, or childcare? How can it be a good thing to have a ministry like a HopeKeepers group for those who live with chronic illness because doesn't that just encourage people to continue to accept their illness, rather than seeking God's will which would, of course, be a healing?

I am very passionate about spreading awareness that "the church" needs to understand more about chronic and invisible illness. Without embracing those with illness, we are missing great ministry opportunities. We must (1) allow healthy people the gift of serving those in need; (2) allow ill people the gift of being served; (3) give ill people the chance to serve others and share the bounty of what God has taught them through suffering.

I have found that people who live with chronic illness understand suffering on a daily basis and are the most compassionate and understanding group of people you may ever know. Oftentimes it is those who live with illness who are the ones trying to make and deliver meals to others who are only slightly more ill than they are. And if you stand outside of a room where a group of people are who have chronic illness but who know Jesus, you'll be pleasantly surprised to hear the joy and laughter that reverberates, even through tears. To live with an illness each day, one can find a sense of humor, true joy in the Lord, and an appreciation for life that was never completely understood before the disease.

Illness will exist, and people can either go through those valleys with great depression that sometimes results in suicide (yes, even believers), or the church can offer what Jesus challenged it to offer: a safe place with food, compassion, and transportation. Luke 14:21 says, "Then the owner of the house became angry and ordered his servant, 'Go out quickly into the streets and alleys of the town and bring in the poor, the crippled, the blind and the lame'" (NIV). I interpret this to mean that we are not just to serve those who are able to make it to church on Sunday morning. Rather, we are to go out into our communities and find the people who are suffering, feeling lonely and disheartened, and bring them into our church so they can see and experience the love of Jesus.

There are many New Age churches that are recognizing this need in the chronically ill of our community, and they are quickly filling it, with transportation to and from church, organized visitation from church members, and more. And for the person who lives with chronic illness, she may be in so much pain, and so desperately want to have some of that pain relieved and to feel taken care of, that despite the fact that she may have grown up knowing Jesus, she may easily be swayed outside of her faith to a different kind of faith, simply because there was a van from the New Age church that would pick her up.

Those involved in church leadership may ask, "Why do those chronically ill people have to be so sensitive? Why do I have to constantly accommodate their needs? Can they not just be grateful that we are doing our best?" The truth of the matter is that people want to be loved and to feel like they are cared for. Most churches believe they are doing this, but those on the receiving end often say that the message or ministry is not clearly being communicated. Simple misunderstandings easily cause frustration and harden hearts. For example, although one may assume that saying, "You look so good!" is a compliment, for the chronically ill person it often feels like the reality of their situation is not believed or that it is invalidated.

Why? This is how it feels: If she looks so good, she can't truly be in that much pain, right? And if she says she is in that much pain, then surely she is just looking for attention, right?

A church can say, "Of course we take care of those who have a chronic illness!" But when a person with an illness needs a ride to the doctor on a weekly basis for six weeks, is the church able to provide for this tangible need? I have found that most churches and individuals have the best of intentions, and it's a lack of communication, not a lack of caring, that causes people to be hurt.

Just comprehending why sending a "Get Well" card may not be the best way to encourage a person who is chronically ill can go a long way in expressing your desire to understand her. It's important to remember that, despite the fact that a person may live with a chronic illness, he still has a life where he is surrounded by all of the happenings that occur in the lives of people who do not live with chronic illness. He may lose his job due to the economy. He may get cancer. His child may be in a car accident. His wife may have an affair. He is not exempt from the challenges and crises of life just because a chronic illness already exists.

The Bible not only admits, but actually assures us, that there will be suffering here on earth. I don't pretend to understand God's reasoning, especially when families suffer through manifold tragedies. However, I do know that He called us to embrace Him during our darkest moments so that when we are ready to go back out into the world, we are able to comfort those who are suffering, regardless of what kind of suffering they are experiencing. This is where 2 Corinthians 1:4 falls into place: "[He] . . . comforts us in all our troubles, so that we can comfort those in any trouble with the comfort we ourselves have received from God" (NIV).

One of the biggest challenges of living with a chronic illness is the daily-ness of it. Every day may be slightly different in the way that it may be a different body part that aches or moves out of place, but the illness never leaves. When we have something like the flu, we are able to put it into perspective, knowing that if we get some sleep, eat some soup, and maybe take some medication, in a week or two our lives will return to normal. When you have a chronic illness, there is no such thing as normal, unless you define normal as "constant chaos." Being able to share my story with others and create an environment where anyone can share his or her story – whether it is an encouraging day or a lonely day – is a great honor. It has allowed me to meet amazing people whose strength I know could only come from a God who promises, "But those who hope in the Lord will renew their strength. They will soar on wings like eagles; they will run and not grow weary, they will walk and not be faint . . ." (Isaiah 40:31, NIV).

During my journey with chronic illness, I have rarely asked for healing, not because I don't desire to be healed, or because I am any kind of a martyr, but simply because I have always believed that God could heal me at any given moment and that He knows that in my heart, I would love to even taste the life "before rheumatoid arthritis" again for a moment. However, I would not want to miss out on the treasures that God may be able to reveal to me only in the darkness.

And there have been many treasures. We became parents through adoption of a newborn baby boy in 2003, and the relationship with his birth family is a gift we never expected. I have a career that I am passionate about and able to do from home, allowing me to work around my disabilities. It also allows me the freedom to be a stay-at-home mom – something I likely would not have chosen, but am forever grateful for.

The blessings I have been given through my chronic illness, from the tangible to the spiritual, are gifts that came in the ugly gift wrap of illness, but gifts I would still never exchange for my health. So, as I take each day and whatever it holds, I cling to what is one of my personal favorite expressions of trust and surrender in the Bible, Psalm 119:50: "My comfort in my suffering is this: Your promise preserves my life."

Questions for personal reflection and/or discussion:

1. If you are a person with a chronic illness, what would you echo or even add to what Lisa has shared in this chapter? Or, if you do

not have a chronic illness, what did you learn that will help you to help loved ones or friends who do live with chronic illness?

2. Lisa wrote: "Sharing one's vulnerabilities and Christ's strength is one of our greatest assets." The Bible says: "That is why, for Christ's sake, I delight in weaknesses, in insults, in hardships, in persecutions, in difficulties. For when I am weak, then I am strong" (2 Corinthians 12:10, NIV). The apostle Paul is describing one of the paradoxes of faith: specifically, that rather than striving for mastery and adequacy in all things, one can entrust to God one's weaknesses, and He turns them into strengths. How have you experienced this yourself or witnessed it in others?

3. Lisa's following thought summarizes the theme of this book: "Telling our story is important. Every person has a story that is unique. If you take ten people diagnosed with the same chronic illness, on the same day, at the same age, their experiences will still differ. And that is one of the reasons that God has given each person his or her own testimony. Regardless of what people may say about your beliefs, they cannot take away your testimony."
Describe the uniqueness of your own personal story in a sentence (or a paragraph of no more than four sentences). If in a group setting, share these thoughts with the group.

4. Do you think that the Christian church could do better in terms of its care for and ministry to people living with chronic illness? If so, what might you do to initiate a dialogue on this question in your own church?

5. Lisa says: "The blessings I have been given through my chronic illness, from the tangible to the spiritual, are gifts that came in the ugly gift wrap of illness, but gifts I would still never exchange for my health." If you were in her situation, would you be able to echo these sentiments? If you are in a situation like hers, and you agree with her, put this expression of faith into your own words.

CHAPTER 9

A WIDOW'S GRIEF AND CONSOLATION
BY DEE BRESTIN

There's an invisible knife sticking out of my heart. My fifty-nine-year-old husband lost his valiant battle with colon cancer. I wait for him to call, to hear his hearty laugh – but silence looms. I long to talk or pray with him about our five children – but he is gone. My body aches to be held by him in the night, but his side of our bed is empty.

I don't particularly like being around Christians who haven't experienced deep suffering. They can be like Job's friends, offering pat answers, misapplying God's truths, bumping up against the knife they do not see. They smile and quote Scripture to me. I cringe. They send a card with a platitude pointing out the silver lining to my pain. I close it quickly. I know they mean well. But they plunge the knife to excruciating depths of pain. Proverbs 25:20 warns: "Singing to someone in deep sorrow is like pouring vinegar in an open cut" (New English Version).

But oh, the comfort of those who have suffered! They understand that it is better not to try to fix the unfixable, but to mourn with those who mourn. There is a Jewish tradition called "Sitting Shiva" that gives us wisdom for how to comfort the suffering. When someone had a catastrophic loss, close friends and family would "Sit Shiva" with them. "Shiva" means seven, which is the biblical number for completion, or, in effect, "as long as it takes to bring comfort." They would come and sit, but not speak unless spoken to, and then only briefly. They would listen to the person share the details of their loss, they would weep, but they would not offer solutions. When author Joe Bayly's child died, he tells of two very different visitors, in his book, *The View From a Hearse:*

> "I was sitting, torn by grief. Someone came and talked to me of God's dealing, of why it happened, of hope beyond the grave.

He talked constantly. I wished he'd go away, and he finally did.

"Another came and sat beside me. He didn't talk. He didn't ask leading questions. He just sat beside me for an hour – or more. He listened when I said something. He listened. He answered briefly. He prayed briefly, and then he went away. I hated to see him go."

During Steve's illness and death, I, too, had wise and unwise friends. The following excerpts from my prayer journal were written the month we received the news of Steve's cancer. The day we received the news, I happened to be speaking at a large retreat in Indiana and had our two daughters with me.

Aug. 3 (fourteen months before Steve's death)
Oh Lord, my girls. Help them. Though many of the women at the retreat were wonderful, surrounding us with prayer, tears, love … some were not so wise. Two sisters cornered Annie (our youngest daughter) and told her how their dad died of cancer and how terrible it was. I guess they were trying to identify with her pain, but she wasn't ready for that. Another quoted Romans 8:28 to her. She turned and fled, breaking through the crowd to get to a back room where she could hide until we could leave. I found her there, crouched in a corner, cold and silent as snow, like she gets.

Oh my Jesus, help.

Aug. 22
We're waiting in the emergency room. Steve had me rush him here due to a blood clot in his leg. David and Lorma came (Steve's partner and his wife). David sat next to Steve, pain etched on his forehead, silent and caring. Lorma put her hand on Steve's heart, tears welling up in her eyes, and prayed simply: "Please God, help."

I can't explain why their pain helped ease our engulfing pain, but it did.

A TIME TO SPEAK AND A TIME TO BE SILENT

The teacher of Ecclesiastes tells us there is a time to speak and a time to be silent. High-tide grief is not the time for words, for trying to explain why God may have allowed this, for attempting to fix the unfixable. I understand why people try to give answers, for I used to do it myself. I would be so nervous around someone whose pain was palpable that I would stammer on, exacerbating their pain. When someone would say:

"At least your children are nearly out of the nest."
I would think: *Oh, they need him. They need him. Don't you see?*

Or:

"It's good he is no longer suffering."
I would think: *Don't you know how much he suffered?*

Or:

"At least you had a wonderful marriage."
I would nod, but think: *Don't you see that's why I miss him so much?*

It was all I could do to keep from screaming. Pointing out the "silver lining" makes you feel like the individual speaking underestimates your pain. That's why it is so much better to simply mourn with them, or to simply say, "I'm so sorry." When someone does that, you feel they are coming alongside and bearing your pain with you – and somehow, that divides the pain.

I did learn to see the heart beneath the words that hurt, that tried to fix. I knew they meant well, even though I wished they would go away. I also learned that when my friends failed me, as they would, for they have feet of clay, there was One who never would, who was acquainted with sorrow, who knew how, better than anyone, to "Sit Shiva."

I also was so blessed to have friends who knew how to "Sit Shiva." They came, they listened, they remembered the anniversary of his death, they prayed, and they brought me the comfort of God.

And when they could not be there, like in the middle of the night, there was One who always sat shiva with me.

THE ONE WHO ALWAYS SITS SHIVA WITH YOU

The following story, which I tell in *The God of All Comfort*, was pivotal in my grief journey:

> One day I was packing up the house to move from a home of sweet memories that I did not want to leave. The littlest things like finding Steve's white surgery coat with his initials, SGB, on the pocket could cause me to crumble.
>
> When I went to bed that night, I was fretful. Though I tried to sleep, anxieties multiplied, leaping over my pillow like bleating sheep.
>
> I turned over on my side, looking at the vacant place where Steve used to be. Oh, my darling – how could this have happened to us?
>
> Steve and I used to call each other "codependent insomniacs." If one of us awoke in the night, he (or she) would whisper to the other, "Are you awake?" When it was me, I knew that even if Steve was asleep, he would rouse to keep me company. If I was worried about something, he would listen to me pour out my heart while stroking my back and empathizing with his deep masculine voice, his calming ways.
>
> Sometimes he would help me laugh about a trouble. Other times, when he knew there was no humor in a situation, he'd simply pray over me and hold me. If sleep still eluded me, he'd start quoting our favorite nursery rhyme:
>
> "Winkin', Blinkin', and Nod, one night sailed off in a wooden shoe; sailed off on a river of crystal light into a sea of

124

dew. . . ."

Safe in Steve's arms, our bed became a wooden shoe sailing off into a sea of dew, and I was lulled to sleep.

But Steve was not there. His side of the bed was achingly empty.

My cry that sleepless night was not nearly as eloquent as David's. I simply sobbed: Help me, help me, help me, God! I knew I needed God to be my Comforter, my Counselor, and my Husband—but that understanding exploded into a question: "But how do I connect with Someone who is not flesh and blood?" When I couldn't immediately sense God's presence, I curled up in the middle of our king-sized bed and wept.

Without even realizing it, I had prayed a prayer of lamentation. The lament, which is modeled in the book of Psalms, is speaking the truth of your sorrowing heart to God. While I was lamenting in that fetal position, a scene from my past came to my mind: I was twenty-one, trying to calm our first-born in the middle of the night. He would awaken, hungry and howling. Though I would run to him and lift him from his crib, unbuttoning my nightgown as we settled in the rocker, he was too fretful to latch onto my breast. He would root about, but if he didn't find me in two seconds, he would rear back, his face red and contorted, his fists flailing. If I stroked his cheek, like the nurse in the hospital had told me to do, trying to coax him to turn toward me, he would erupt in anger, bursting into a horrific wail, one that I knew carried through our thin apartment walls. A mother's breasts respond to her baby's cry, and my milk let down, ready for my baby—but his fretful state kept him from connecting with me. I kept thinking, *I'm right here, I'm right here!* A very long ten minutes later, he'd finally find me and nurse greedily. His perspiring face would relax, his eyes closing at half-mast in contentment. I would think, *Oh my, Pumpkin, what was all that about? I was right here.*

Suddenly, I identified. I was that baby, concentrating more on my distress than on the One who was right there. I sensed the Lord saying: Dee, I am right here. I am right here.

Gradually, my soul began to calm, my body began to relax, and my eyes went to half-mast.

When I woke the next morning, much more rested, I opened my Bible to pray through a Psalm, as was, thank God, already my habit. My Psalm that morning "happened" to be Psalm 131. When I read it, I knew that God was "kissing me." ("A kiss from the King" according to rabbinic tradition, is a living word from God.) God's living Word was confirming to me exactly what I had experienced from His Spirit the night before.

> I have stilled and quieted my soul;
> like a weaned child with its mother,
> like a weaned child is my soul within me.
> Psalm 131:2 (NIV).

In my journey of grief, I have learned how to still and quiet my fretful soul with the truth, truth often found in the ancient book of Psalms. Dietrich Bonhoeffer, a German pastor who was martyred for trying to stop Hitler, explained that prayer is more than simply pouring out our hearts to God. In order to find our way into the arms of God, whether our soul is full or empty, we need the very words of God. When I pray using my own words, I often feel like I'm rowing upstream, getting nowhere. But when I pray using the Psalms, I catch the wind of the Spirit. Likewise, I often use great music, based on the Psalms, to still my soul. For nearly a year, every night, I sang "Be Still My Soul." This song, paired with the calming melody of Finlandia, soothes the savage breast. Music and truth paired together help me still and quiet my soul, like a weaned child with its mother.

Like so many suffering saints from the past, I discovered the power of praying the Psalms of lament. This holy prayer journal echoed the pain of my soul. The Psalms of praise stuck in my throat, but the Psalms of lament helped me avoid backing away from God, my only lifeline. They freed me to be honest with God, for the Psalms reminded me to avoid the trap of dishonesty with

God as we bring to Him "what is in us, not what ought to be in us."

God wants honesty from us because He wants intimacy with us. Not only the psalmists, but Jeremiah, Job, and Jesus lamented in prayer. The lament helps you hang on to God when you do not understand what He is doing, to accept the mystery of suffering. Again and again in the Psalms of lament, I would see that, hidden behind the psalmist, was Jesus. Here is the One acquainted with grief, equipped, better than anyone, to "Sit Shiva." In the Psalms of lament I spied Him as He cried out:

> My God, my God, why have you forsaken me?
> Why are you so far from saving me,
> So far from the words of my groaning?
> Psalm 22:1 (NIV).

> My bones suffer mortal agony,
> As my foes taunt me,
> Saying to me all day long,
> "Where is your God?"
> Psalm 42:10 (NIV).

Jesus is equipped to "Sit Shiva" when our friends fail us. We do not have a high priest who is unacquainted with sorrow, but we have the Man of Sorrows, who is close to the broken-hearted, who mourns with those who mourn.

Questions for personal reflection and/or discussion:

1. If you have experienced a catastrophic loss, such as the death of your spouse, which group of "comforters" did you appreciate most – those who came and seemed to be unable to stop talking, or those who came to be with you without saying much? Explain your answer.

2. The biblical character Job lost all his wealth and all his children

and also his health. When his friends came to comfort him, they sat with him for seven days without saying anything, because they saw the depth of his pain. Read the story in Job 2:11-13. But then, Job started venting his emotions, starting by cursing the day of his birth. After his lament in Job 3, his would-be comforters became his critics (read on if you wish). If this type of thing has ever happened to you, describe it briefly, say how it felt, and then try to figure out why previously good friends can criticize or even judge a person in such anguish.

3. Dee Brestin's story is heart-wrenching and hopeful, at the same time. She and her husband loved each other very much. If you think that the degree of one's pain in such a loss is related to the degree of one's love, prior to the loss, what would you say to her a month after the funeral?

4. The Psalms of lament became a comfort for the author during the long, dark nights, and also as she tried to find her way beyond the darkness of grief. Read aloud one or more of the passages that she cites, or, better yet, find a Psalm of lament in your Bible that captures how you have sometimes felt in the past. Read this aloud as a prayer to God, or share it in the same way with your group.

5. The author has been able to emerge into the light of life again and has developed a ministry to the broken-hearted. Do you think this result is unique, extraordinary, or simply what anyone who has experienced significant loss can achieve if he or she will keep walking by faith?

CHAPTER 10
MEDICINE AND NARRATIVES

The influence of people's stories, and the forums by which they are permitted to share their narratives, are an integral part of society, catalyzing health in all its dimensions: physical, emotional and spiritual. Most health care providers use only a small, albeit important, aspect of treatment when dispensing the products of medical science. Yet the astute clinician and other caregivers realize that a patient's social supports, his attitude about his contributions and meaning, and his desire to persevere or survive represent formidable yet intangible remedies. And it is clear that these therapeutic factors are dispensed in the everyday telling or acting out of one's story. Oftentimes, the physician has the occasion to hear a piece of a patient's story. If missed, a great portion of the remedy will be lost to the technical aspects of dispensing medicine. One can receive a drug but not understand the human factors that will make the difference between illness and health. Dr. Rita Charon has championed the work of narrative medicine as she observes the power of the story in treating patients. Her illustrative medical narrative is that of Ms. Lambert.

Dr. Charon writes: "Ms. Lambert (NOT HER REAL NAME) is a thirty-three-year-old woman with Charcot-Marie Tooth disease [a neurological disease causing loss of muscle activity in arms and legs]. Her grandmother, mother, two aunts, and three of her four siblings have the disabling disease as well. Her two nieces showed signs of the disease by the age of two years. Despite being wheelchair-bound with declining use of her arms and hands, the patient lives a life filled with passion and responsibility. 'How's Phillip?' the physician asks, on a routine medical follow-up visit. At the age of seven years, Ms. Lambert's son is vivacious, smart, and the center – and source of meaning – of the patient's world. The patient answers, 'Phillip has developed weakness in both feet and legs, causing his feet to flop when he runs.' The patient knows what this signifies, even before neurologic tests confirm the diagnosis. Her vigil tinged with fear, she has been watching her son every day for seven years, daring to believe that her child might escape her family's fate. Now she is engulfed by sadness for her little boy. 'It's harder having been healthy for seven years,' she says. 'How's he going to take it?' The physician, too, is engulfed by sadness as she listens to her patient, measuring the magnitude of her loss. She, too, had dared to hope for health for Phillip. The physician grieves along with the patient, aware anew of how disease changes everything, what it means, what it claims, how random is its unfairness, and how much courage it takes to look it full in the face."[1]

In the reading of this narrative, one readily identifies the emotions of fear, sadness, and grief that accompany the diagnosis of a familial disease that is beginning to show up in a seven-year-old son of the patient. However, as the story is being told, the thoughts and meanings connected to this diagnosis are also unveiled. Raising this, until now, healthy child, was the center of the patient's life, who was herself wheelchair-bound with the same illness. His "escape" from the ravages of this illness, which had afflicted two nieces much earlier in childhood, became, to the patient's mind, a greater obstacle to adaptation. A hope became a burden. Denial becomes a dreaded reality. With three generations of what appears to be good enough coping among the many family members afflicted with this neurologic illness, the questions and issues emerged again with new nuances individual to the storyteller who is also the patient.

When the physician writes down the narrative and shows the patient what she has written, treatment takes place. Certainly the physical aspects of the illness have not been ameliorated, but the cognitive and psychological distress have been remedied with the infusion of empathic understanding of the narrative. With the vast numbers of chronic illnesses and patients who have to bear them, this form of healing is a valuable commodity in the medical armamentarium. Such narrative healing can be readily administered not only by the doctor, but also by the many ancillary supports in a patient's life.

"Perhaps the most effective methods to strengthen professionalism in medicine are to endow physicians with the competence required to fulfill their narrative duties toward one another: to envision the stories of science, to teach individual students responsibly, to give and accept collegial oversight, and to kindle and enforce the intersubjective kinship bonds among health care professionals. Only when physicians have the narrative skills to recognize medicine's ideals, swear to one another to be governed by them, and hold one another accountable to them can they live up to the profession to serve as physicians."[2]

The stories physicians tell about themselves and each other fulfill the obligations alluded to by Dr. Charon. I (Dr. Eng) am deeply affected by the narratives of other physicians and healers, particularly those who have served on the mission field. From the time I was in college, I have been fascinated by the adventurous and sacrificial healers who have gone overseas to serve the kingdom of Christ by serving humanity.

If one were to select a single Westerner who knew the Chinese people, their hopes, and their fears, one would not hesitate to mention the late Dr. Edward Hume.[3] Having lived twenty-five years in China as a medical missionary, he contributed as greatly to the growth of Western medicine in China as the Chinese people richly added to his understanding of their culture. Dr. Hume left us many accounts of his experiences in the East, and being the multi-faceted person he was, his writings discuss not only medicine, but the prospects of Christianity in the Far East, the political attitudes in China, the impact of nationalism on the Chinese people, and many other aspects of China in which he took an interest.

Edward Hicks Hume was born on May 15, 1876, in Ahmednagar, India, and raised in Bombay where his missionary father Edward Sackett Hume taught in an Indian school. The Hume tradition in India had been established two generations earlier, when Edward's grandfather, Robert Hume, set sail with his young bride, Hannah Derby Sackett, on a ship destined for India. Edward Sackett and Robert Wilson were both born to them during their missionary service in Bombay. However, when their father took sick and ultimately died on a return trip to America, Hannah took the responsibilities of raising her sons for missionary work, and ultimately sent them to Yale. Edward Sackett Hume graduated in 1870, married Charlotte Chandler, daughter of an Indian missionary, the Reverend John Chandler, and together they set sail to India as missionary teachers.

When their eldest, Edward Hicks, was born, he was already the product of two generations of harvesters in the mission fields of the East. Therefore, he and his family naturally assumed that he would maintain the fine work of the Hume's in India. There were no physicians in the Hume family as far as they could recall. Edward's interest in medicine blossomed when he was a young child in Bombay. At the age of twelve, he and his father paid a visit to an American hospital in Madura, India, where young Edward, strongly touched by the gentleness and care Dr. Van Allen showed his Indian patients, decided he would study medicine. Following in his father's footsteps, he attended and graduated from Yale University, whereupon he received the following momentous letter:

Dear Hume,
Your father writes me from Bombay that you are going to study
medicine. Of course you are coming to Johns Hopkins.
(Signed) William H. Welch

Edward accepted the offer of his father's close friend, embarking upon a venture that was to elevate him to the class of the most highly trained and prestigious physicians America could produce.

Hume's stay at Hopkins was as typical as any student's experiences who happened to study under the remarkable corps of now famous physicians like Osler, Halsted, Welch, and Kelly. Owing to his close relationship with Dr. Welch, Hume learned the ideological and administrative skills of medical education that later aided him in the establishment of a medical school in China. From Halsted, Kelly, and foremost from Osler, he not only acquired the excellent medical expertise which he later applied to treating his Chinese patients, but developed a sincere human quality as a

best, and that He would provide for the future of her loved ones. We may think we are not ready, that our work on this earth is not done, but God may have other plans.

She read the New King James Bible and did a study on her favorites. The passages that spoke to her especially were 2 Timothy 1:7: "For God has not given us a spirit of fear, but of power and of love and of a sound mind," and 2 Corinthians 12:9: "And He said to me, "My grace is sufficient for you, for my strength is made perfect in weakness." Therefore most gladly I will rather boast in my infirmities, that the power of Christ may rest upon me."

Finally, she memorized Philippians 4:6-7 "Be anxious for nothing, but in everything by prayer and supplication, with thanksgiving, let your requests be made known to God; and the peace of God, which surpasses all understanding, will guard your hearts and minds through Christ Jesus."

She tried to keep her focus on God and not on her circumstances. Whenever fearful thoughts would intrude on her peace, she would quote her Bible verses or play uplifting hymns and praise songs. In fact, she sang softly on the way to the operating suite the song, "Great is thy faithfulness, O God my Father. . . ."

Are the trials over? A second nodule was found by the left upper lung three months later. Was it missed on the previous CAT scans or was it a new nodule? Only time will tell, but for now God has plans for her to be here.

Alison La Frence, MD, echoed similar convictions as she shared her own story about dealing with a chronic illness that forced her to retire from her family practice of medicine. She wrote:

That clinic day ten years ago, was like so many others. I was over-booked and running late. The teenager in the next room, however, was memorable. She was pregnant and abortion-minded. As I held her hand and the tears flowed freely down her face, she poured out the emotions she had struggled to keep at bay over the previous several weeks. The ten-minute appointment soon stretched into an hour, as I became aware of my lack of counseling skills in this area. I left the room and looked up the number of the nearest Crisis Pregnancy Center (CPC). After talking with the director of the ministry about their services, I sent the young woman over to the center for assistance. I kept this patient in my prayers that entire week.

I took care of this teenager throughout her pregnancy, and delivered her baby. On her post-partum visit, I asked about her experience with the CPC. Smiling, she shared with me examples of the physical, emotional, and spiritual ways she had received support. For me, this experience opened the door to the life-saving world of pro-life ministries. After finding out how few physicians in this area were involved, I jumped in with both feet and have never looked back.

A decade earlier, my physician-husband and I had busy practices and an enjoyable life. We were healthy, financially stable, and we were thinking of having children. As Christians, we had gone on several short-term medical missionary projects and were planning on future trips. We were both content, when the walls around us came tumbling down.

In August 1995, I woke up in an ambulance. In an ER in Wisconsin, I was told that I'd had a grand-mal seizure while attending my family reunion. Thankfully, the CT of my head was normal. After a night of observation, I was discharged home.

Over the following nine days, I became quite ill and was once again hospitalized, this time with the diagnosis of viral encephalitis. Except for the unremitting, intense pain in my head, I remember very little of that first month.

My bout with viral encephalitis caused three separate thorns of affliction in my life and resulted in a chronic disability. One way or another, each thorn pricks at my flesh on a daily basis.

My first thorn is my seizure disorder. I had numerous grand-mal seizures between 1995-1996. On multiple medications, I have remained seizure-free since that time.

Migraine headaches are my most troublesome thorn. These headaches occur every two to three days, despite seeing multiple specialists and utilizing numerous treatment modalities.

The third post-encephalitic thorn is the most devastating. I cannot overstate the negative impact of this injury on my life. However, I am also eternally grateful for this weakness. For it was this thorn that led to the process of my spiritual healing.

Soon after recovery, I noticed difficulty with my speech and language (i.e. short-term memory, word finding, math). I developed coping skills and, unless I had a headache or was tired, my deficits were not too obvious. When the headaches became a daily event, in late 1998, my impairments became more evident.

I took a leave of absence from work and saw a pain specialist, who ordered a neuropsychological test after observing my problem with communication. Taking this exam brought tears to my eyes as I (who had previously graduated near the top of my medical school class) was now shown the full extent of my cognitive disability.

The test showed mild diffuse brain damage due to the encephalitis. My previously bruised self-esteem took an incredible beating. I felt like a broken physician, unable to help others, because my problems were beyond fixing, even by God. I attended a brain injury clinic in the summer of 1999. One-on-one classes were personally designed to maximize my abilities. To accomplish this, I first had to acknowledge my deficits. I also needed to open the door again to the Lord's grace and healing power.

In 1999, I was asked to join the board of directors of one of the local CPCs. As a Christian, I considered this offer both an incredible honor and an opportunity for service. However, my thorns were weighing me down like a mighty ball and chain. Instead of being filled with happiness, becoming a member overwhelmed me with a feeling of dread.

That year, both my self-esteem and my communication skills were at the bottom of the barrel. I had just started new medications for my headaches and, though feeling better, the side effect of significant fatigue was quite problematic. My first inclination was to decline the board's offer. However, my speech pathologist encouraged me to reconsider. After prayer and discussion with my husband, I accepted their invitation.

For the first several months, I said only a few words per meeting, until my confidence improved. By the end of the first year, I was talking in sentences with this godly group of individuals, who had now become my friends. A remarkable event happened at the end of my second year (2001). The board president moved away, and a new election of officers was held. I was elected vice president of the board. A physician, full of thorns, including difficulty with communication skills, was now the vice president of the board of a Crisis Pregnancy Center. I remember thinking at the time: *I am so thankful that the role of vice president is a backup position on the board (only to fully function if the president was incapacitated or died). Therefore, I will not have to do a lot of talking with this commitment.*

I was quite mistaken, because our Lord had different plans in mind. Over several years, my association with this CPC (and several others) led to the recovery of most of my language skills.

For the next few years, I volunteered in multiple aspects of the pro-life ministry. I did this as my health allowed and, most importantly, as led by our Lord to do. In the past, I had been a busy Christian physician who placed a high value on her intelligence. How else could I have gotten through medical school? A disabling illness, the thorns of which wounded my most valued asset, brought me to my knees. Our loving Lord reached down and healed my soul by intertwining my life with that of the unborn.

Through suffering, I have learned so much. The most important lesson, however, is that HIS GRACE IS SUFFICIENT FOR ME.

These stories demonstrate the importance of narrative in medicine. Patients tell stories important to their treatment. Doctors have reactions to these stories that affect their role as healers, whether it be positive or negative. Finally, doctors have stories of their own which profoundly influence and inspire others. These stories benefit their colleagues, students, patients, or society in general.

Questions for personal reflection and/or discussion:

1. Do you agree that it is a good thing that doctors in training are being taught how to engage their patients in dialogue that goes beyond their primary symptoms to matters of the heart and mind? If

in a group setting, role-play a doctor-patient dialogue that would prove encouraging to the patient, and possibly even to the doctor.

2. When you've been ill, did you find it helpful in your recovery to be able to share your personal narrative with others, not just how you became ill, but how the illness was affecting you emotionally, socially, and even spiritually?

3. Dr. Hume and his wife were extremely committed to fulfilling what they saw as a mission from God. When you compare yourself with people of such high ideals and character, how do you feel? If in a group setting, share the first word that comes to mind. Do you think that God also uses "regular" people?

4. Doctors learn a lot about the patient perspective when they become patients themselves. If you had to choose a doctor to attend you in a serious illness, would you prefer one who has never been ill, or one who understands serious illness due to personal experience? If in a group setting, explain your answer.

5. Both women doctors, whose stories were included, reached the conclusion that God's grace was sufficient for them. If you have ever struggled with something and then found solace in that same concept (which originated with the apostle Paul), share the circumstances and how this conviction has helped you.

NOTES:
1. Rita Charon, 1900 JAMA, October 17, 2001—Vol 286, No. 15 (Reprinted) ©2001 American Medical Association.
2. Ibid.
3. The account of Dr. Hume's ministry through medicine was written by Dr. Elaine Eng, as part of her senior thesis at Princeton University. Background material included primary sources at Yale Divinity School and the Yale in China Program (now known as the Yale-China Association).
4. Author unknown.

CHAPTER 11
CHRISTIAN WOMANHOOD

Opportunities for women to tell their stories have existed throughout history. These include writing, composing songs or poetry, and the many verbal exchanges that occur at gatherings of women all provide opportunities for storytelling. Stories are passed from generation to generation as in the example of the song "I Love to Tell the Story." Regarding the author, Katherine Hankey, 1834-1911:

> "Katherine Hankey was 32 years old when she wrote the hymn 'I Love to Tell the Story.' It arose out of a deep desire in her heart to tell the simple gospel story wherever she was in life. First, it was in the Sunday school of Clapham, England, where she became a devoted, refined, consecrated woman. Then, it was in the heart of Africa, where she spent most of her life, giving the sales of all her writings to missions. Finally, it was in the hospitals of London, where she spent the last minutes of her life telling lonely patients of God's beautiful love. When Katherine Hankey wrote 'I Love to Tell the Story' in 1866, she was doing more than expressing a feeling in her own being; she was projecting that same feeling into the minds of thousands of people through the years who would sing her song and receive the same challenge."

> I love to tell the story, Of unseen things above,
> Of Jesus and His glory, Of Jesus and His love.
> I love to tell the story, Because I know 'tis true
> It satisfies my longings, As nothing else can do.[1]

Settings for the sharing of trials, joys, and emotions supported by a foundation of Scripture, prayer, and caring abound in women's ministries both within the church and in the large organizations that support the concerns of Christian women. The spectrum of life events and issues that affect women and their families are numerous. This chapter will attempt to address some of them through the stories told by women meeting in a weekly Bible study. Hopefully, this will help you see how storytelling can enrich your experience in similar settings, and help you learn to deal with these life events.

We will begin with Janet's story of her pregnancy. As we hear Janet's story, I'll use her narrative to explain the medical aspects of having a child, to give us a glimpse of God's power and the beauty of His design.

Janet's Story: Pregnancy

At age forty-three, Janet found herself to be pregnant with the long-awaited baby she had almost given up on. A mother of two, she had always wanted a big family, but a stillbirth and a first trimester miscarriage followed by five years of trying had dashed her hopes. Then one day she realized that she was three weeks late for her period. She felt nauseous. She didn't have the usual appetite and enthusiasm for food that she, as a red-blooded Chinese-American woman, normally had. An active member of her women's Bible study, Janet often relished the dishes that she and the other women prepared. She was careful about nutrition, but enjoyed preparing healthy foods like soups, chicken dumplings, and soy milk products.

She could always be counted on to locate the healthiest and finest grocery items. Since her husband was in the food industry, she had a keen instinct about what was tasty as well as healthy. So, this nausea and lack of appetite was unusual, but it did not dampen her spirits, as she knew it meant that her dream was coming true. Once the pregnancy was confirmed, she kept the news to herself until the fifth month. During that first trimester, she didn't gain much weight, but did the best she could to rest and maintain good eating habits. Her second trimester was much better, and she felt energetic, even more so than other non-pregnant women in the congregation. She helped serve in the church activities and enjoyed her condition.

Then, in her thirtieth week, she developed premature labor and was put on medication and confined to bed rest for the rest of her pregnancy. For many women, this would be a major inconvenience and sacrifice, and, with two other children, a major challenge. But she calmly resigned herself to this, telling herself that each week of bed rest would help the baby and allow it to grow bigger in her womb. She kept to a schedule of reading, watching some TV, and praying to the God whom she had trusted and to whom her father had introduced her. How she managed this while being on the medication to prevent early labor was no mean feat, and only a loving God would make this go as easily as it did for Janet. In fact, the final delivery was the easiest of her deliveries when, to her surprise, a baby boy of almost nine pounds was delivered without any problems. What a cause for rejoicing!

Let's imagine we can look into how the Lord has made Janet in order to prepare her for pregnancy. Pretend you have just been lowered through a tiny incision into her abdominal cavity. Whoa, look out! It's slippery in there with the small and large intestines rolling around; in fact, many feet of them are moving around in waves, ushering the processed food molecules to their destinations. Just what are we looking at today? Oh yes, the female reproductive system – that part of Janet responsible for procreation. Let's head south in the abdominal cavity and look for two small organs found there. They look like two pale sponges – sometimes speckled with one or more pea-like swellings called follicles. These follicles contain one of Janet's eggs surrounded by cells that produce the female hormones needed to help the egg mature. Once the egg matures, it is released from the ovary in a process called ovulation. Look! Our timing is perfect! The left ovary just released a ripened egg. This only happens once a month. Now, the finger-like projections from the two fallopian tubes go into action. The left tube is grabbing onto the egg and moving it down into the tube where it will travel for a few days. If it by chance meets up with a sperm cell swimming up the tube, fertilization may take place. But if there is no sperm (i.e. if Janet has not had intercourse in the past four to five days or she doesn't in the next day or two), then the egg will just disintegrate in the tube.

God has designed women in such a dynamic way that many series of events have to take place in order for pregnancy to happen. Let me describe this: Each month is divided into twenty-eight to thirty days depending on the length of the woman's menstrual cycle. Day #1 is defined as the first of her menstrual period, which represents the shedding of the unused uterine lining, a sort of monthly house-cleaning, if you will. As the days go by, the brain realizes that no pregnancy has occurred in the past month, so, in order to try again for conception, it sends out messengers called "follicle stimulating hormone" (FSH) and "luteinizing hormone" (LH) to tell the ovary to start maturing one or two eggs that are lying dormant. A follicle starts to ripen as the surrounding cells, under the influence of FSH and LH, begin to produce their special hormones, estrogen and progesterone. These in turn stimulate the uterus to develop a rich lining in preparation for a potential pregnancy.

The uterus is a pear-shaped muscular organ sitting inside the pelvis. As I mentioned, the tubes that carry the egg after it ruptures from the ovary in the abdominal cavity are connected to the upper lateral pole of the uterus; thus, the egg, if fertilized, can enter the uterus through the tube. So on day #14, "ovulation" takes place. This means that the ovary releases the egg. The egg travels through the tube to the uterus in the hope of meeting up with a sperm.

Meanwhile, the follicular cells in the ovary are cranking up hormones, particularly progesterone, which causes the uterine lining to become more and more plush, making it a perfect bedding in which a fertilized egg can implant. Just when the small ovarian follicle has produced as many hormones as it possibly could, the implanted egg and sperm, which we now call the zygote, will take over and make its own source of hormones, one of which is "human chorionic gonadotropin" (HCG). The cells making HCG will eventually become an organ, which will turn out to be the placenta. This organ will make sure the baby gets all its nutrition, hormonal supply, and resources from Janet in order to grow and develop in the next nine months. Such complicated events are all going on inside Janet without her realizing it.

Her first clue to any changes is when she doesn't have her period at the usual expected time. A pregnancy test, which measures HCG, the hormone that is made by placental cells, indicates, when positive, that Janet is "with child." If there is no pregnancy, then she will have her period at the usual time after day #28 or 30. How remarkable this menstrual cycle is that potentially leads to pregnancy. The symphony of hormonal and anatomical events is finely orchestrated and conducted by a wise and creative God.

> "For You formed my inward parts;
>> You covered me in my mother's womb.
> I will praise You, for I am fearfully and wonderfully made;
>> Marvelous are Your works,
>> And that my soul knows very well.
> My frame was not hidden from You,
>> When I was made in secret,
>> And skillfully wrought in the lowest parts of the earth.
> Your eyes saw my substance, being yet unformed.
>> And in Your book they all were written,
>> The days fashioned for me,
>> When as yet there were none of them."

(Psalm 139:13-16, NKJV)

Fay's Story: Menopause

Fay, aged fifty-three, has served on short-term missions to the Navajo people almost every year for the past eleven years. She has enjoyed watching her three daughters grow and mature from this experience develop responsibility in caring for others, especially the Navajo children. She states that they have developed from very young children to mature, responsible teenagers without her telling them what to do. She has learned a great deal about other people, including the cultural differences of the Navajo, as well as an understanding of her missionary teammates. And, in fact, she has learned much about herself in the process. She states that she was very naïve about people and spiritual things prior to her trips, but that she gained much wisdom in the process.

Fay began experiencing perimenopause in her early forties, as it manifested itself with some mild symptoms of emotionality, periodic insomnia, and irregular menses. She states that she coped with the irritability by taking time out and disciplining herself to remain self-controlled in relation to her children. She says that the time reminded her of her teenage years when she felt anxious and worried about how others viewed her. She said she was so self-absorbed that she thought others were watching her and judging her when, in fact, she realized that they were oblivious to her because they were involved with themselves. She realized that she should not interpret others' behavior personally, as it often wasn't meant that way. Later in life, she used the same approach to deal with the emotions arising during menopause.

A major coping factor Fay used was to learn as much as she could about different stages in a woman's life, and relevant health issues. She researched menopause in order to prepare herself. She states that she read many books, some more informative than others, but felt that in the end, what she learned was very helpful in dealing with, and even decreasing, her symptoms. She has a good approach to healthy living, exercising, and eating a healthy diet. She has chosen not to take hormone replacement therapy, and she feels very comfortable about her decision, having adjusted well to menopause, this despite having had a hysterectomy and removal of her ovaries. She thanks God for her easy transition. She thinks that more women would be helped through this stage of life if they had support and education groups in the church, but menopause is rarely discussed in churches.

Since her girls are getting older and will be leaving for college soon, she says, "I can make plans for the rest of my life." After all, she tells her daughters, "I have dreams, too." She hopes to travel, especially to visit missionaries around the world. Visiting Alaska is also a dream for her. Praise God for this planner.

It is important that women's groups in the Christian community address this issue by helping women share their stories in order to improve their outlook, their sense of worth, and to gain support with health issues.

Sara's Story: My Only Son (Multiple Miscarriages)

Married at age twenty-four, Sara wanted to enjoy life with her new husband for a few years before having children. However, as five, and then seven, years passed and they did not conceive, she began to wonder what was happening. And then, she had three miscarriages in a row, all within the first two months of pregnancy. Her pain with the first miscarriage was all the more acute as she watched other mothers continue in their pregnancies and have their children.

The second was worsened by the fact that her mother implied that she was doing something wrong. By the third miscarriage, she was beside herself and did not think she could repeat the process anymore. Then, when medical tests showed that she had one chromosome that was shorter than normal, she was told that her children were at greater risk for genetic defects. When she became pregnant for the fourth time, she was in agony, worrying about whether or not she would miscarry, and if she did not, whether the child would be born defective. She also did not want to think about the prospect of an abortion that her doctor recommended if there were any abnormalities.

She could not keep these thoughts out of her head. She felt very alone and frightened, and recalls the day that she went into the doctor's office crying, petrified to learn the amniocentesis results. Thankfully, they were normal, and Sara went on to have a healthy baby boy at seven and a half months.

Shortly after this, Sara met some Christian women in the neighborhood and started to attend their Bible study. Eventually, she became a Christian and joined their church. She became pregnant again and asked one of the women to help her with her son. Again, despite the all too familiar restrictive routine of bed rest, she had a fourth miscarriage, followed by another one. But by this time, Sara had begun to believe and trust God for her life. She states that although she wanted very much to have another child, she prayed that she would accept God's will if it was His plan for her to have only the one child.

After this prayer, she was at peace with herself and thankful for the son that God had given her. She knew that God had given her a new perspective on this, and that He cared for her. She remembers the emotional and physical pain of the many miscarriages, especially the loneliness she felt, despite having a very supportive husband who took great care of her. She says that the experience has taught her to be sensitive to children and their needs. She also believes that being a Christian has taken away much of her loneliness.

Although the miscarriages will always be a difficult thing to forget, she believes that had she been a Christian at the time, she would have gained a lot of support from the Christian women with whom she fellowships now. She states that they would have provided opportunities for her to talk about her situation. She wants to share her feelings about this struggle because she feels that, unless you go through it, you may not understand.

> "Praise be to the God and Father of our Lord Jesus Christ, the Father of compassion and the God of all comfort, who comforts us in all our troubles, so that we can comfort those in any trouble with the comfort we ourselves have received from God" (2 Corinthians 1:3,4, NIV).

Like Sara, many women experience pregnancy losses, which can occur in a number of ways. Some women experience multiple miscarriages, a stillbirth, or the death of a child due to congenital abnormalities. These events impose much stress on a woman and her husband. Their reactions to this include many of the symptoms of grief, such as anger, sadness, denial, and shock. Their grief is not only for the loss of the wanted child, but a loss of their immediate dream of a family. Some feel that they have been "left behind," especially when they see that their friends have gone on to start families. They often dread Mother's Day and are upset when they see other mothers with children.

Loneliness is a strong feeling among women who have had pregnancy losses. And so, there is often a need for support groups to

152

help women and couples in this situation. Bethany Christian Services has a ministry called "Stepping Stones," designed to assist women with pregnancy loss or infertility. They provide newsletters, an online bookstore, conferences, and resources to encourage support groups among women. They can be reached at:

Stepping Stones
C/O Bethany Christian Services
901 Eastern Ave. NE
PO Box 294
Grand Rapids, MI 49501-0294

But Sara's story does not end here. When her son was in high school, he approached her and stated in earnest that he wanted to join the Marines. This was during the time period following 9/11 and the war on terrorism, and the USA was actively engaged in battle in Afghanistan and Iraq. Sara's heart was stricken with worry at this, and she did whatever she could to dissuade him. Coaxing him to give college a try and then re-evaluate gave her only a temporary respite. After three semesters in college, he left school to begin his training as a Marine. This tried Sara's faith so much, and she struggled as many in her church encouraged her with Scripture, prayed for her, and listened to her worries. She turned to many other women who had children entering the Marines and communicated with them by phone or e-mail. She pleaded with government and military officials to protect and advocate for "my only son" to be spared of the dangerous work that he had entered. But the day when she got word that he was going to be deployed to Iraq, she was faced with her worst fear. There was no longer anything she could do but trust God and let go.

"How do you do that?" she asked. There aren't many who can answer that question easily. How can you surrender your fears when the only son you bore after so many losses will now be placed in a war? As Sara reflected on this difficult phase of her motherhood, she recalled the biblical teachings that helped her the most, such as Philippians 4:6-9:

"Do not be anxious about anything, but in everything, by prayer and petition, with thanksgiving, present your requests to God. And the peace of God, which transcends all understanding, will guard your hearts and your minds in Christ Jesus. Finally, brothers, whatever is true, whatever is noble, whatever is right, whatever is pure, whatever is lovely, whatever is admirable – if anything is excellent or praiseworthy – think about such things. Whatever you have learned or received or heard from me, or seen in me – put it into practice. And the God of peace will be with you" (NIV).

Infertility – Soraya Cina

Infertility is a hard road that many women and their husbands have to negotiate. We see it in the Bible in the lives of Hannah, Rachel, and Sarah. Here in her own words, a Bible study member wrote about her journey, which she entitled "They Say, I Say:"

From its onset three years ago, till now, my journey through infertility has been and continues to be a growing process. I have wept, cried, sobbed, mourned, grieved, questioned, and wondered. My faith in God has been tried. My friendships have been tested. And, by the grace of God, my relationship with Him has been nurtured toward a deeper trust and a more serene hope in His sovereign will. My life is in His capable, loving hands, and I have resolved to live my life to the fullest for Him.

But it hasn't been an easy road. Many times, being barren implies being a failure, a disappointment, being defective, being abnormal. Being barren is not celebrated, welcomed, understood, or approved. Being barren usually translates into "being incapable," "lacking," or "there is something wrong." Words, meanings, interpretations, and assumptions have all played a heavy role in my journey. Words have been both arrows and arms. They have been wounding arrows when they have been the ill-timed, poorly-phrased well wishes and questions from well-meaning friends and family. They have been the loving arms of my Heavenly Father when they have been His perfectly timed, excellently phrased promises and words of unchanging, everlasting love.

And in the stillness of my times with my Caring Father, when I retreat and recover from the wounds of words, I am on my way to healing:

"Lord, they say I don't have a child because I don't ask You for one."
"Child, I say I know you and your needs before you ask me."

"Lord, they say, with impatience in their voices, 'When will you be a mother?'"
"Child, I say, my timing is perfect."

"Lord, they say I should have a child already because I have been married for awhile."
"Child, I say, my ways are higher than man's ways."

"Lord, they say I have not tried hard enough to have a child."
"Child, I say, I am the One who opens and closes wombs."

"Lord, they say, with their eyes and faces, 'What are you doing wrong?' 'Why can't you conceive?'"
"Child, I say, I know what I am doing and I have a plan for you."

"Lord, they say, 'Try this; it worked for her: it could work for you.'"
"Child, I say, do not fret; trust me; be still; I am God."

"Lord, they say, 'Life is passing you by; many others who have come after you already have many children.'"
"Child, I say, my plan for you is to prosper you and not to harm you, to give you hope and a future."

"Lord, they say, 'When will it be your turn to be a mother?'"
"Child, I say, I know what's best for you."

"Lord, they say, with sad eyes and looks of pity, 'What will you do now?'"
"Child, I say, I am your source of hope and joy. I am the One who gives meaning to your life. Child, they say many things and will say many more things that will hurt you and disappoint you. Set

your eyes on me; I am the Author and Perfecter of your faith. I am your Creator. I am your all-in-all. Put your trust in me. I know the best for you, and I will show you the way to it. I have come that you may have life and have it to the full. I myself have come to the world to redeem you and make you a part of my family. I love you. Let not your ear be attentive to the world's cries, but listen to me. I have always loved you. No part of your life is unknown to me. I will unfold my precious plan in your life, in my perfect time, in my powerful way, in beauty. Wait on me, Child. I have promised to be with you, and I will come through."

And once more I see that my barrenness is not a surprise to Him, nor is it an accident of nature, but it is His sovereign act of love and purpose for this life of mine redeemed with His incredible love.

And once again, my heart rests in His bosom, and is comforted and cared for, and the wounds of words are gently touched and healing.

And one more time, I thrust my life into His hands and resolve to live it to the fullest, to the praise and glory of my Loving Redeemer."[2]

Questions for personal reflection and/or discussion:

1. When have you been the recipient of wounding words?

2. When have you been the giver of wounding words?

3. What words does God give you when you feel lonely or inadequate?

4. How can you encourage a friend struggling with infertility, miscarriage, menopause, or other specifically female issues?

5. How might a support group focused on these issues be helpful?

Notes:
1. Helen Salem Rizk, *Stories of the Christian Hymns* (Abington Press, 1964) p. 25.

2. Personal communication from Soraya Cina.

Chapter 12
The Story That Transforms –
The Gospel Across Cultures

" Jesus saith unto him, I am the way, the truth, and the life: no man cometh unto the Father, but by me" (John 14:6, KJV).

This chapter will look at the interaction between the gospel and the cultural aspects of personal narratives. The narratives chosen come from several different continents, and though there are many possible issues to examine, I will underscore only a few salient points. Namely, that the Christian gospel can be culturally contextualized as revealed in narrative; that the gospel stands on its own as distinct despite culture; and, finally, that the gospel has the ability to restore the relationships broken by the adverse events sometimes witnessed in the culture and environment.

The first narrative takes place in Japan. It is a story about Toyohiko Kagawa: "Born to a Buddhist family at the end of the nineteenth century, young Kagawa became a Christian through the influence of two Presbyterian missionaries who had opened their home to high school students wanting to learn English. Disinherited by his family following his conversion, Kagawa attended Meiji Gakiun, a Presbyterian college in Tokyo. While there, his Christianity took on a strong social conscience. . . .

"*Across the Death Land*, one of Kagawa's first published books and one of his all-time best sellers, was, interestingly enough, a novel. He deeply desired to make following Jesus Christ an option for Japanese people, and narrative writing was one of his means to reach this goal. He chose to use the most popular genre of his day, the autobiographical novel. Although the novel was fiction, it was 'fiction' that told Kagawa's own story of disillusionment, conversion, and subsequent dedication to living in the slums and ministering God's love in that situation. . . .

"Kagawa followed the aesthetic standards of his society. *Across the Death Land* demonstrates Japanese values of suggestion (showing the gospel through story rather than telling it directly). He used the communication styles and values of the people for whom he wrote. Narrative becomes a means of mission – a way of learning about a culture and listening to its people, and, as Toyohiko Kagawa demonstrates, a way of being in a culture and of communicating at a deep level the truths of God's saving grace to that culture."[1]

The narrative of Iichi, the male protagonist in the book *Across the Death Land,* is told in the thoughts, observations, and dialogue with Iichi himself. This young man was torn by the Japanese imperative to honor his father, and describes his own rebellion and disgust toward his father, the mayor of the town, due to his penchant for immorality and oppression of the poor. This insatiable appetite for heartless self-indulgence was not only at the expense of the townspeople, but also at the expense of his own family, including Iichi. Perhaps because of Iichi's exposure to the gospel through attendance at the Christian school, or perhaps because he was imbued with his own strong sense of right and wrong, or perhaps because of his identification with the victims, Iichi disavows, in stages, his father's idols of money, sex, and power.

The first step for Iichi is his growing sense of existential ennui in returning to his father's household after being away for school. He plods through the daily existence, participating in Japanese observances, but he remains disconnected emotionally. He moves to the second stage of searching for alternatives and is attracted to Tsuruko, a lovely young maiden who has adopted Christian values and beliefs after attending church. Iichi is devoted to her because of her faith and her willingness to listen to his struggles. Iichi also searches for alternatives through diligent reading of philosophy and Christian theology.

The most dramatic stage of his story's evolution is when he actively makes a break from his father after having a serious argument, marked by emotional outbursts and a physical altercation. Thus breaking the Japanese code of honoring parents, Iichi leaves his home to discover a life of living true to himself, his pursuit of his faith, and to realize his mission to serve the poor and oppressed.

These stages are revealed in his experiences and travels in the various towns of Japan. His story is an odyssey of emotions, physical journeying, and spiritual development. But most importantly, this journey is a thesis on cultural contextualization of the gospel of Jesus Christ. Does the gospel ever stand alone in this context? Given the subtlety of the author's style, it may be hard to identify, but accounts such as the following passage demonstrate that the gospel stands alone and distinctive, despite cultural influences.

"Besides these there was Tsuruko, who was seated on the other side of the table listening to the pastor. The pastor preached very earnestly. Sometimes he appeared to be addressing himself to the grave-looking workman; the next moment he had fixed his eyes on Iichi and was preaching to him. Outside, a jinrikishaman stopped and two or three people gathered. The pastor was earnestly telling the story of Jesus and Nicodemus, and his eyes were lit up by his fervour. The 'rikisha' made a creaking sound as the 'rikishaman' departed, and at the noise Tsuruko lifted her head for a moment and looked out into the street.

"The sermon was a long one, lasting an hour. When it was finished, the girl took her place in front of the organ, and the married woman with a taste for drink opened her eyes and then abruptly rose and departed. Then came the concluding hymn:

> There is a fountain filled with blood,
> Drawn from Immanuel's veins;
> And sinners plunged beneath that flood
> Lose all their guilty stains.

"Listening, Iichi felt in his heart that he also had become a follower of Jesus."[2]

The novel's narrative demonstrates the reparative power of the gospel in broken lives. Having ruptured the relationship with his earthly father and all its repercussions, Iichi has found a heavenly God who is the impetus for his life's work. Since this book is an autobiographical novel, it is clear that the author Kagawa, himself, accepted faith in Christ in a similar way to direct his own life's mission.

Run Baby Run, a film about Nicky Cruz, a man caught in the gripping snares of two powerful cultures, shows the unique integrity and power of the gospel to reveal itself as a distinct and superceding element in a person's narrative. Born in Puerto Rico to a leader of a powerful witchcraft cult, Nicky experienced torturous and cruel beatings from his father, employing the sadistic tools of their worship. He graphically describes his childhood screams for help as his father tossed him, bound, into a cage where the pigeons used for the bloody rituals were kept. He tells how the birds furiously pecked at his little body. Young Nicky experienced this cruelty from his father in the name of religion and the need to discipline him. At age ten, he was sent alone to New York City to experience the hostile ghetto, a drug-infested culture of extreme poverty and isolation. He coped by joining a notorious gang. In this setting, he lived exposed to much violence and excelled in street fighting, proving himself to be one of the most vicious and dangerous leaders of the gang.

It was not until a white preacher from Pennsylvania, David Wilkerson, came to New York to preach the gospel to the street gangs that Nicky heard about the love of Christ. Repelled by this alien religion which spoke of a God, and not knowing whether this deity might or might not bear any resemblance to the witchcraft demon of his father, Nicky initially reacted with hatred. He directed his anger toward this preacher and reviled the narrative of love portrayed by Jesus. But it did not take long before this new story of Jesus entered into Nicky's narrative, superseding and usurping the cultural influences that had penetrated so deeply into the young man.

As a result, he went from being a street gang brawler to being one of the most influential pastors in recent history. Paired with the Rev. David Wilkerson, they developed the powerful ministry known as Teen Challenge, which addresses the generation of teens affected by drugs, loneliness, and gang culture. The transformation of Nicky and the many young people saved from their broken lives through this ministry dramatizes the unique power of the gospel to displace culture.

Finally, the gospel can create peace in the narrative of those affected by the wounding effects of culture and environment. The following is an example of such a narrative. Chia Lin Yu, a missionary serving in the Republic of Congo, writes the following account of Mama Jeanne:

"The story of Mama Jeanne reminds me of Jesus' encounter with a Samaritan woman at the well (John 4:1-26). Jesus was talking to this lonely woman about being thirsty and finding that which quenches the thirst of her heart. Jesus was thirsty for the water that could quench His physical thirst, but this woman was thirsty for something much deeper at her soul level. The turning point in this intimate conversation is, I think, when Jesus tenderly invites this woman to go and call her husband and then to come back to Him. 'I have no husband,' she replies. Then Jesus says to her, 'You are right when you say you have no husband. The fact is, you have had five husbands, and the man you have is not your husband. What you have just said is quite true.'

"What a gentle confrontation with a soul that has lost its most cherished dream! Jesus knew her secret desire and her broken dream. She just wanted to be loved and cherished. She went from one relationship to another, hoping to find true love. But after five marriages, she has bitterly given up any hope to be happily married, settling for something less than what God had wanted for her.

"Mama Jeanne is like this Samaritan woman who longs to be loved and married, but she ends up living a life which is not what she wanted. Jeanne Berthe Loumba was born and grew up in a village in Dolisie, in the Province Niari, Republic of Congo. When she was seventeen, she fell in love with a young man. She was studying nursing in a professional school in Kinshasa, Zaire (Democratic Republic of Congo). When this young man went to her family to ask permission to marry her, her uncle, the brother of her mother, refused to give her to him. In the south of Congo, the children belong not to their birth fathers but to the brother of their mothers. The young couple had no choice but to obey the decision of their parents. Jeanne was so broken-hearted and angry at her uncle that she began to live a life of disorder as an act of vengeance against her uncle. When she was nineteen, still in the nursing school, she met a guy and had her first child. Then she met another man who was already married. They fell in love. After he did the first presentation of dowry (asking the permission and the list of gifts and bride price from the family of the bride), they moved in together and had three children together. But since this man never had the intention to complete the state marriage and the church marriage, Jeanne left him and had a child with another man. Before she encountered Christ and accepted Christ as the Savior and the Lord of her life, she had had five children, two miscarriages, and two abortions. She had had sexual relationships with six different men, yet she had never been married. But ALL SHE EVER WANTED WAS TO BE MARRIED, TO BE STABLE, TO BE LOVED.

"She is now in her sixties, a wonderful and beautiful Christian woman who serves as a deaconess in one of the CMA churches in Brazzaville, Congo. None of her five children has an intimate personal relationship with Christ, though they all accepted Him when they were young. Her youngest son is in the military and is a drug addict. He sometimes breaks into her house and steals all her things to buy drugs. Although she worked as a nurse in a middle school until her retirement, she has not been able to receive her pension for four years. Even now she struggles to get her pension because of the corruption in the government. She suffers arthritis and she doesn't have the money, the health insurance, or the social security to help pay for her treatment. None of her children is helping care for her needs. She lives by herself.

"There are many young women in Congo facing challenges that are even greater and more complicated than those of Mama Jeanne. The problems of AIDS, abortion, traditional sexual practices, pornography, Western cultural influences, urbanization, political corruption, unemployment, prostitution, poverty, sexual harassment on the campus and in the society, the role of women and attitude toward women in the Congolese culture – these are some of the difficulties that a young Congolese woman faces. In Congo, it may take ten years for a couple to complete their marriage project: 1st stage: presentation of dowry to the family (cultural tradition); 2nd stage: state marriage (legal in the eyes of the State); final stage: church marriage (blessing from God). Many of them have never finished their marriage project. Premarital sex, divorce, abandonment, abortion, adultery, multiple sexual partners, polygamy among the rich people, prostitution, etc. result in a large population of 'Fille-mère' (single teen moms), and put the entire youth population at high risk of AIDS.

"Mama Jeanne told me her story with great peace and gratitude to Jesus, who loves her with everlasting love. She has learned to trust the Lord to face her daily struggles and to serve people with a joyful heart. I did not sense any bitterness in her, though I detected regret and traces of sorrow on her face from time to time as she was telling me her concerns for her grown children. Life has been hard for her, but I have never heard her complaining against God. She is a woman who was in touch with her brokenness as well as with the healing presence of Lord Jesus Christ in her journey to wholeness.

"Mama Jeanne is a woman of integrity who serves God faithfully as church treasurer. Culturally speaking, financial need that occurs first has the first claim on the available resources. If something is not being actively used, it is considered available Congolese are obligated to share their resources with needy family members and relatives. Because Mama Jeanne, being a poor old woman, had access to the church's money, she could have been easily succumbed to social pressure to help herself and her family with God's money. Such practice is unfortunately fairly common in Congo. Her trustworthiness, however, has been confirmed and appreciated by her community.

"I remember that she once brought me a bag of potatoes which cost about 2,000 cfa (equivalent of four US dollars). I remember it because it was a lot of money to her. She could have bought food for two to three days, taken buses thirteen times, or purchased medicines for her arthritis, but she chose to buy potatoes and gave them to me. Congolese do not usually eat potatoes. They are too expensive; and only the 'moudeles,' meaning the white people, eat them. I was so touched by this thoughtful gesture. During my time in Congo, many people had approached me and befriended me because they wanted money or things from me, but this poor old Congolese Christian woman wanted to give me something. I admired her not just because she had a grateful heart but also because she did not let poverty nor disappointments in life destroy her dignity. She has given me more than just potatoes, she has given me friendship and respect. She has opened her heart to me and treated me as her sister in Christ."[3]

The narratives in this chapter illustrate the idea that the gospel story causes transformation in a person's life despite ongoing cultural and environmental injustices. The resolutions offered in these narratives are internal and spiritual, oriented toward peace and healing. Yet the reader can appreciate the cultural and environmental context in which this occurs. The adaptation and coping seen in the narratives can change the meaning of a person's life. The external problems may continue to exist and plague both men and women. Will the gospel impact the narratives as well as the conditions of these people? There are many who believe so and will make many sacrifices to prove it so on the mission field.

Questions for personal reflection and/or discussion:

1. How do you think the woman's encounter with Jesus in John 4 changed the narrative of the rest of her life?

2. What cultural or environmental factors form a tight grip on your life?

3. The gospel is valid across cultures, as shown by the stories in

this chapter. Cultures can be local, regional, national, or international. If you have tried to cross these barriers, share your experience(s).

4. Some of the characters in this chapter have given up much to follow Christ. Most of them might say that they only did what following Jesus required. If you have had conflicts or challenges in this arena, describe them and how you resolved them.

5. Has Jesus entered and changed the narrative of your life? How? See John 14:6.

Notes:
1. *Footprints of God: A Narrative Theology of Mission.* Editors: Charles Van Engen, Nancy Thomas, Robert Gallagher. M.A.R.C Publishers, division of World Vision, 1999.
2. Kagawa, Toyohiko. (1925) *Before the Dawn.* (Revised title) I. Fukumoto and T. Satchell, Trans.) London: Chatto and Windus. Original work published 1920, page 90.
3. Personal communication by Chia Lin Yu.

CHAPTER 13
FROM PAIN TO JOY AGAIN
by David B. Biebel, DMin

"Daddy, if I was killed, would you still be able to find me?" As we rode along together in the summer of 1978, I had warned Jonathan not to lean against the car door because he might fall out.

As usual, he had asked a series of questions beginning with "Why?" and I had tried to explain that if he fell out he might get hurt. In fact, he might be killed.

This prompted his simple inquiry. Perhaps it was the sheer pain of the idea that prevented my response. Just the thought of Jonathan's being taken away was something I could not handle.

So I never answered him.

I wish I had. I also wish I had prepared him more fully for what he was about to face. I thought there would be time. He wasn't quite four years old, still too young to be able to understand the deeper things about life and death and God. There would be time, I expected, for all of that.

There wasn't.

During the last few days of August, 1978, Jonathan was stricken with what appeared to be a virus of some sort, the main symptom of which was unrelenting nausea. We waited for the symptoms to abate so our lives could return to normal.

Concerned with the severity of our son's illness, my wife took him to a doctor's office on Thursday, August 31, where an examination revealed he had what seemed to be a case of tonsillitis. With that diagnosis and a shot of penicillin for Jonathan, my wife and Jonathan returned home. We were somewhat relieved, expecting that Jonathan would soon become his normal self again.

He never did.

Late the next morning, I received a phone call at the office at the church I pastored. My wife was crying. "Davie," she said, "will you come home and see if you can get Jonathan to talk right?"

Rushing home, I found Jonathan lying quietly on the couch. I urged him to talk to me. "Jonathan, can you talk to Daddy?"

He didn't answer.

I called the rescue squad, fumbling for words to describe Jonathan's condition. I said something about our having trouble getting a response from him. They were there within minutes.

Back in the living room, I sat next to our little boy. His teeth were clenched tightly and his breathing was labored, but he was conscious. "I want a drink," he murmured. Sitting him up, I tried to help him drink.

With the promise that I would be close behind, my wife and Jonathan left with the rescue squad for the hospital, which was about thirty miles from our small town in northern Michigan. For some reason, perhaps because we were already in shock, we didn't recognize how sick Jonathan was. The worst we feared was that he might be in the hospital overnight or that he might have to undergo a tonsillectomy.

Upon my arrival at the hospital, I was relieved to find that our doctor suspected a slight case of pneumonia. An oxygen tent, antibiotics, and time would take care of that.

After stopping in the room briefly to let my wife know I was there, I wandered to a nearby restaurant to pick up a little lunch for us. It was a meal left unfinished.

When I returned, my wife was trying to comfort Jonathan, who was lying under the clear plastic oxygen canopy, his teeth and hands clenched more tightly than before. He was having difficulty breathing, taking great deep breaths, and blowing them out through his lips with a vibrating noise. He was still conscious, but, I think, terribly frightened.

The nurse tried to reassure us as we became increasingly alarmed about Jonathan's condition. Finally, another doctor was called in.

Surprised at the critical condition of our son, and quickly assessing the situation, the new doctor said, "This boy's in trouble!" What we had feared was true. Immediately, he was transported by ambulance to Milwaukee, Wisconsin, a high speed two-hundred mile journey for Jonathan and his mother. I stayed behind to try to get things in order, before leaving to join them later that day.

The hours passed slowly on Monday, September 4, as we waited expectantly. Gradually, Jonathan's wakefulness increased. He seemed alert, following movements in the room with his eyes. He recognized characters from some of his favorite story books.

But he couldn't talk to us. Except for repeating the barely understandable sentences, "I want mommy" and "I want to go home," which he had said the day before, he uttered only an occasional guttural cry, often accompanied by a bilateral movement of his arms and legs.

Tuesday there was more of the same. Though we attached undue significance to the fact that he was moving and making sounds, our doctor began to talk more and more about the possibility – in fact the likelihood – that an "insult to the brain" had occurred.

"Insult to the brain" is a medical way of describing what we feared more than anything else – brain damage. The thought was overwhelming, almost devastating. Yet there was still no diagnosis, and Jonathan was alert, so we clung to our faint thread of hope.

We had to. Without it we might have been destroyed. With all that Jonathan had been – athletic and intelligent – the thought that his brain might have been damaged was incomprehensible. He could hit a plastic golf ball, hit a baseball, throw his foam rubber basketball consistently through a hoop. He could speak well and enjoyed playing with other children. From our perspective, he had everything going for him. Now we were being told it might be gone.

With the probability of brain damage increasing each passing day, I plunged into a deep despair. And the only way I could stay sane was to write. I had to write. Somehow I had to let the geyser of pain find expression, or I knew I would surely implode.

So I started a journal, which later became the foundation of a book. It was the best way available to me at the time to save the story and also to share it with others. This is adapted from the first entry:

Dear Jonathan,

As I begin this letter, I'm sitting here in the intensive care unit of the hospital waiting for you to regain full consciousness. We don't know the reason for this sudden illness that has so radically changed our lives and threatened yours during the past forty hours. Perhaps by the time you are old enough to understand what I am trying to say in this letter, this whole thing will be cleared up completely.

I love you so much, Jonathan, that it is impossible to put it into words. If there were only some way for me to bear the pain and to protect you from the traumatic experience you are now having – even to the point of taking your place – I would do it gladly.

Just the thought that you might be taken from us, Jon, the thought that you might die, filled me with such sorrow and heaviness of heart that it was almost impossible to bear. Only God Himself knows the meaning of my tears and my prayers. As I thought about losing you, my son, I could not even imagine how I might carry on – especially in my public life – without you.

How thankful I am that God understands my doubts, doubts regarding the outcome of this in spite of the faithful prayers of so many…. How thankful I am, too, that He understands my fears and my heart's initial rebellion, as I considered my options should you die: How could I ever preach again? How could I ever do another funeral, especially yours? Do I really want to be in the ministry (a question I've been wrestling with lately)? It's such a constant pressure to have to live a public life all the time, to be an example.

If I should forget to focus on the positive things of the ministry in years to come, Jonathan, I'll be doing you a great disservice. [So] as I look ahead, no matter what happens in this I know that I must fulfill His calling if I want real joy and a sense of fulfillment in my life. To be able to translate this experience – how can I ever do that? – into some kind of ministry to someone else, that is the goal.

There are so many things I would like to share with you in the coming days. I've been thinking, even before you got sick, of the day (perhaps soon) when you will be able to grasp with a child's faith what it means to have Jesus in your heart and life. Almost since you started to talk, His name has been often on your lips.

Jonathan, since you were very young I've been planning to write you this, and perhaps record it – three and a half years go so fast! – to tell you of my extreme joy, my happiness when you were born, to tell you of how much I have learned about God the Father by becoming a father myself. Thank you.

I wanted to tell you, because I grew up somehow thinking otherwise about myself, that with God's help you have the potential and abilities, the physical and mental equipment, to do or to be anything you want to do or be.

If I had written this then, I would have told you how we chose your name – Jonathan – "whom God gives," after a friend, John Aker, and because Jonathan was a friend of David and I want you to be my friend.

Hearing you cry out, and whispering in your ear, "Daddy is here; you don't have to be afraid," reminds me of how God so often tries to get that message through to me. But I don't listen, either because I can't hear or because I don't want to.

It seems unbelievable to me that as you became seriously ill and we brought you to the hospital, I was in the final stages of preparing a message on Philippians 4:6-9, where God gives His cure for anxiety. But that is the way He is, because He sees ahead of us. Instead of my preparing the message, He was preparing me for this.

As I finish this letter you are still resting comfortably. We're all hopeful that in the next few hours you will regain your strength and your consciousness. And I trust that with time your normal vigorous health will return.

Who knows what the future will hold for any of us, Jonathan? We have no guarantee about it, except some Scripture promises and the unfailing love of God, which we know will bring into our lives exactly what is best for us, including the beginning and the end. For He is the Alpha and Omega, the beginning and the end, worthy of our worship, honor, and praise.

Someday, son, this letter may help you understand a little of what is going through my mind as I sit and wait by your side, and it will be a reminder to me that I want to share these feelings of my heart with you more often.

Someday, if the Lord allows it, we may walk together down some backwoods road or float down a wilderness river or camp together in a Rocky Mountain meadow and enjoy more fully this kind of communication and communion with God and with each other. That is my goal for us as I think of our relationship tonight.

So my son, my love, my pride and my joy, sleep on. But then awake, I pray, to regain all that you were. If I could protect you from the pain of these next few days, I would do it. But we must pass through it together, as through any trial, like a river, to get to the other side.

"And we know that God causes all things to work together for good to those who love God, to those who are called according to His purpose. . . . For I am convinced that neither death, nor life, nor angels, nor principalities, nor things present, nor things to come, nor powers, nor height, nor depth, nor any other created thing, shall be able to separate us from the love of God, which is in Christ Jesus our Lord" (Rom. 8:28,38,39 NASB).

With love,
Your Dad

As those first days became a week, and then another week, many people would try to encourage me, to lift me up, sometimes exhorting me to a deeper faith and trust in God's purposes. But it was nearly impossible for me, being face to face all day with Jonathan's desperate situation, to communicate his condition to anyone positively, much less optimistically.

Of course, everyone wanted to hear something, anything, that indicated progress. Miles away and unable to do much more than pray for us, our family and friends didn't want to hear a despondent, pessimistic message. Only one person we called regularly truly accepted me, without a hint of judging, whatever my message or my attitude might be. At times even he gently exhorted me to rely more fully on my faith.

Others were sometimes less than gentle in urging me to "practice what I preach," since I was a pastor by profession. What they were saying was true, but I was in no condition to respond to that truth. Our faith had been sorely tested. Still, flimsy as it was, it helped to sustain us. We also had hope, and although it too was damaged, my hope was still that Jonathan would recover. We waited by his side tenaciously, sometimes almost hovering over him, watching for any sign that his capabilities were returning.

Late at night I was watching Jonathan's lips tremble as well as his shoulder and arm. I cried. I hoped it was purposeful. In retrospect, I suppose we must have impressed the hospital personnel as being almost neurotically optimistic, the way we were poised protectively near him, studiously pointing out every little thing that might be of significance. But to have done less would have been a betrayal. During those mid-night hours, I wrote this poem:

COME BACK

Come back, my son, from the black,
The Canyon's edge, the dreadful deep
Sleep, fearful, fitful, unnatural,
Restless. Wrestle back to me.

Come back from the muddy brown
Unknown, uncommon wilderness.
Escape that prison camp, make war
Again, a foray into consciousness.

Come back, today, through the gray
Fog. I pray you will still see
And know and feel and be, to me,
A break-through sun, burning into day.

Return, I shout, through the haze,
To run and cry and laugh and play.
Come back from that dark, lonely night.
Crash softly into life's warm light.

173

We grasped at any thread of hope, although our level of hope rose and fell depending on which medical person we were with at the moment. We believed we were seeing a gradual improvement in Jonathan's condition. His hands and legs were gaining strength, and some strength was returning to his neck muscles, which had been almost entirely powerless.

We kept a record of his progress, as we were determined to capture every positive sign. We recorded that he was using the muscles of his forehead and eyebrows more, and that he had yawned several times, occasionally, immediately following someone else's yawn. Hearing him sigh after yawning, we wondered if his larynx was returning to normal.

Even when he was sleeping, we watched and waited, noticing that the tremors we had seen when he was awake were perhaps even more pronounced then, especially in his arms, legs, feet, and toes. It seemed that once during the afternoon he reached for a small paper figure that I was about to put into his hand.

We didn't know what to look for, nor did we know who or what to believe. Gradually, the cacophony of convictions and emotions began to take its toll on both of us, and I became exhausted.

Imperceptibly, yet relentlessly, spasticity was taking control of Jonathan's limbs. To combat the growing tightness of his muscles, he was getting regular attention from the physical therapy staff. Although the exercising increased his irritability, the physical and visual stimulation helped him to stay alert.

Not only had he lost control of his limbs, but he was having trouble controlling his salivating. Because of that, one of the physical therapists began to call him "Droolpuss." A professional should have known better.

In my identification with Jonathan and his struggle, I felt that his new limitations must be humiliating to him, in light of his former capacities. Perhaps it was a projection of my own inner turmoil, but to me the therapist's new label represented the ridicule Jonathan might have to endure throughout his life. It made me fighting mad, and in that one aspect of identifying with him, I began to experience what many parents of handicapped children live with for years.

How long would it be, I wondered, before Jonathan would begin to make some measurable improvement? How long before he would be able to feed himself and communicate? How long before he would be freed from his awful bondage? How long would it be until our lives could return to "normal"?

The pressure that these speculations placed upon us was intense. I wondered how (or even if) we could stand it. Beneath an appearance of strength, I found myself quite weak in the face of the potential ordeal ahead, though I was learning more about patience and compassion than I could possibly have learned in another type of classroom: Patience is learned by having to wait. And compassion is learned by having a broken heart.

Upon the recommendation of a friend, and with the prospect of taking Jonathan home without a diagnosis or a prognosis with his significant limitations, we took him to the Mayo Clinic in Rochester, Minnesota. We thought that a few days of testing and analysis there would provide some of the missing pieces in the puzzle of Jonathan's illness. At least we might receive some idea of its cause, and what we could expect in the future.

Secretly we were hoping for a miracle cure.

That first night we met a pediatrician doing his residency in neurology. Gently he reviewed with us Jonathan's medical history, probing for any helpful information. Several times during that initial interview, the doctor made statements like, "You know how sick he is, don't you?" as he did some simple tests, tapping and investigating, trying to assess our son's condition.

I don't think we really did know how sick Jonathan was. Thinking his situation had stabilized, we had been prepared to take him home. We expected improvement, however gradual. We still hoped he would recover. Our trip to Rochester was at the same time an expression of that hope and an integral part of it. From a psychological perspective we were practicing denial, because we were unable to cope with the severe emotional distress that an admission of the sobering reality of Jonathan's condition would bring.

Of the many other statements the doctor made that first night in Rochester, one stands out dramatically for me due to the simple fact that I cannot remember it! It was repressed immediately. All I remember is that something he said caused me so much pain that my mind refused to register his words.

We were encountering a traumatic reality when we had hoped for something optimistic. Even the doctor's simple suggestion that a catheter be used to avoid the irritation that wet diapers would eventually cause met with my internal resistance. I couldn't face the implications of even such a simple procedure.

Amazingly, the next morning, before I left Rochester to return to my home in Carney for the weekend, the doctor announced that he had an opinion regarding the cause of Jonathan's condition. At last, we thought, a diagnosis! But he wouldn't reveal his theory to us, he said, until after a battery of tests that would be made in the next few days.

My plan was to return to Rochester when the testing had been completed, to bring my wife and Jonathan home. In the meantime, I would spend time with our daughter, Allison, as well as try to catch up on some church work.

Also, I was eagerly, and somewhat selfishly, anticipating a few days of hunting. Up before dawn the next morning, I enjoyed immensely the crisp October morning as I hunted deer a few miles from Carney. I lingered awhile before returning to the home where I was staying.

Gene and Bruce Peterson intercepted me on the road as I was returning, and followed me back to the house. I expected that they wanted to talk about hunting or church matters. But Gene got right to the point. "Pastor," he said, "I have some bad news for you. Jonathan has died."

Those were the hardest words I have ever heard. They're permanently etched in my memory.

Stunned, I cried out, "Why?" and wandered back to the side of the van, fighting the tears. After all we had been through, still the end had come without any warning, as a terrible shock.

Amidst that shock, we had to do all the things that bereaved parents do – choose a casket, clothes for him to wear, flowers, and, in my case, what the services would contain, since I was the pastor of the church where the first service was held (there were two – one in Michigan, then another for friends and family back in New England). Hundreds of people attended, and we steeled ourselves against the awful fatigue and drain of having to comfort them, in one way or another.

Thousands of words were shared, only two of which I recall, since people really don't know what to say when they don't know what to say, and most are not wise enough to simply be silent. But the words I recall were from Johnny Palmer, a special friend who, as he began to weep upon the sight of Jonathan in that little casket, hugged me and said, "I'm sorry."

After traveling to New England, we laid Jonathan's body to rest near my parents' home in New Hampshire, the scene set against the breathtaking autumn beauty of early October. But the brightness of the day provided a real contrast to the darkness settling over my soul.

Standing near the head of his casket, I committed Jonathan's body to the ground. "Forasmuch as the spirit of this loved one has departed, with cherished memories we therefore commit his body to its resting place, Jonathan ... JAH NATHAN ... the gift of God. The Lord gives and the Lord takes away ... blessed be the name of the Lord."

I had to say the words myself. "Ashes to ashes, dust to dust." I dropped the petals of a red rose over the head of the gray metal casket, secretly wishing I could throw them. I doubt that anyone noticed how angrily I tore those petals from the little rose. Everyone there was probably impressed with my strength, my composure, my faith. But I was angry, deeply hurt, and plunging into a depression that, except for infrequent moments of affirmation and faith, would last for months.

In one sense, the struggle was over. In another sense, it had just begun. Perhaps its most significant and debilitating aspect was guilt. It feels like this: The courtroom is hushed. The defendant stands as the verdict is pronounced: "Guilty. Guilty as charged."

"Guilty. You are guilty!" So often the verdict booms out, echoing through the judgment halls of our own minds, where the court is always in session and the prosecutor, judge, jury, and defendant are all one and the same – our Self.

Guilt is a potentially destructive and tremendously motivational force. It transformed my life for months, reducing me to a point of relative ineffectiveness and making me a slave to my past. While it is true that parents of children who die often experience guilt and remorse, in my case the struggle was intensified by the pathology report we received in November. The tests showed that the brain injury appeared to have occurred as a result of blockage of small blood vessels, and it was suspected that this resulted from a severe state of dehydration and sludging of blood flow in some of the small blood vessels of the brain.

If dehydration were the cause, then we were at fault for not properly caring for Jonathan. The weight of this new guilt crushed me emotionally. It seemed there was no escape. There could be no rationalizing it away. There was nothing anyone could say to help.

One scene was etched indelibly on my mind. I remembered getting up with Jonathan in the early morning hours of September 1, 1978, as he struggled with nausea for the fourth straight night. Standing at the bathroom sink on his little stool after the nausea had subsided, he asked me for a drink.

I told him no. I thought his taking in anything would only make him worse. He believed me. He trusted me and obeyed me, although his body was undoubtedly crying out for water.

Later, a doctor told us that one small drink each half hour is an effective safeguard against dehydration. We had been so ignorant as parents, so poorly prepared to take care of our children.

Deep down in many of us there is a nagging fear that life is all a cosmic joke, existence without meaning, and we are a race of helpless, hopeless creatures crying out without effect against blind fate. So the angry protestations of one who is in the grips of a deep sorrow can threaten those who are not; his lament could be a faint hint that the existentialist is right and that faith is all wrong.

Another source of fear may be that the affliction of an apparently righteous man contradicts the common belief (or hope) that right living merits God's protection. These kinds of fears could be a major reason that well-meaning comforters often fail to provide the true comfort of God to a hurting and somewhat rebellious mourner. Through ignorance, a potential comforter may end up judging or rejecting the person who needs his help.

In our day of simple formulas for spiritual success, some would try to limit grief to the realm of the purely spiritual, rather than allowing it to be what it is, a reaction that permeates a person's existence on every level. Painting it all in spiritual terms makes the problem of grief much easier to deal with for potential comforters, for the bereaved can now be exhorted to get himself straightened out with God and everything will be all right.

To do this, however, the bereaved must play a game with himself emotionally, physically, and spiritually. His depression isn't demon possession or oppression. Rather, it is simple, barefaced sorrow in the process of being worked through. A person in deep sorrow, despair, or despondency makes his comforters not only afraid but also uncomfortable. So the comforters may exhort the bereaved to try to act or speak in a manner inconsistent with his true feelings.

The return to joy takes time. In the midst of sorrow, a smile need not be forced. The wound takes time to heal. But how difficult it is for some comforters to allow the bereaved that time!

In the fall of 1978, I received a phone call late at night in relation to what seemed to the caller to be a crisis need of another. Would I come and try to help? At that point I was an emotional wreck myself, and I said so. I said I couldn't come. I was having enough problems handling my own emotional turmoil and didn't want to add to it the turmoil of another. Later the comment was made, "He should have been over it already."

I struggled on for another couple years in that little town, torn between my commitment to serve the Lord and His people, and my relatively unsuccessful attempt to mend my own broken heart. Then the district superintendent paid a visit, to inform me that his perspective was that I didn't have a "pastor's heart." Not surprisingly, not long thereafter, we moved away and moved on.

Ultimately, God is the true source of all the comfort we receive. He is with us in all our tribulations – ready, willing, and able to meet our needs and to comfort and quiet our hearts. His objective is twofold. Primarily, it is to help us in our time of need. But He also has in mind others to whom we will be able to minister in His name precisely because of, and not in spite of, our experience.

Because of our suffering, we are able to empathetically identify with another person experiencing similar distress (although we should never assume or say we know how that other person feels, because of the unique nature of grief). Still, having gone through something similar, we can understand far better than most others how the person may be feeling or what he or she is struggling with.

We will not have to seek opportunities to minister in this way, for those in distress who know about our loss will seek us out. Since Jonathan's illness and death, hundreds of people have shared their very personal sorrows with me.

There was the woman whose daughter has taken care of an invalid son for years. There was the mother whose young son lost a battle with leukemia. There was the woman who experienced a psychotic break when she came upon the scene of the automobile accident in which her husband was killed, only ten days before she gave birth to a son. The list, through these thirty-plus years, has become very long, and the pain we've shared with others has taken us very deep into the pit of their despair. Each new story shared brings a new perspective on our own losses, and in addition, a certain kind of joy, the joy that comes with seeing God use us for His good.

Joy can arise from trials. "Giving it your thoughtful consideration," says James, "the perspective of faith can bring complete joy, even in the face of a very great trial." He doesn't say "trials are joyful." The point is that by faith we can realize that through our trials God is making us more like Christ. In this we can rejoice, for that kind of growth is certainly a good thing.

One of the turning points for me in my journey through grief toward joy occurred when, a few months into the process, I found Isaiah 61:1-3, and I realized that as a result of losing Jonathan, I had found my true calling:

The Spirit of the Lord GOD is upon me,
Because the LORD has anointed me
To bring good news to the afflicted;
He has sent me to bind up the brokenhearted,
To proclaim liberty to captives
And freedom to prisoners;
To proclaim the favorable year of the LORD
And the day of vengeance of our God;
To comfort all who mourn,
To grant those who mourn in Zion,
Giving them a garland instead of ashes,
The oil of gladness instead of mourning,
The mantle of praise instead of a spirit of fainting.
So they will be called oaks of righteousness,
The planting of the LORD, that He may be glorified (NASB).

Since then there have been many twists and turns, and also many opportunities to fulfill that calling, for we are surrounded by many brokenhearted, wandering, and wondering folks, who long for a word of encouragement and a reason to hope – that there is any meaning in it all, or even that life is still worth living.

When we have hope, firmly linked to faith in a trustworthy God, and we give ourselves to those who hurt, we are doing what Jesus would do if He were here, in the flesh, today. And when I think about it that way, I know without a doubt that although I could do much worse, I surely can do no better than to share that hope with others, for as Peter wrote, we should be always ready to share the reason for the hope that is in us, with gentleness and respect (see 1 Pet. 3:15).

If you have faced inexpressible adversity, this calling is an open invitation to you, as well, not only from me, but more importantly, from the One who created you for a purpose. Keep walking by faith, through the sorrow and the darkness, and in time you will echo the words of Dante, who, having emerged from the dark depths of hell, sees "the shining world," and says, "And so we came forth, and once again beheld the stars" (The Divine Comedy: Inferno, Canto 34).

And it won't take writing or cowriting nearly twenty books, or starting a publishing house like I've done, but it will most likely be one-to-one, and also in a group setting, where some of the best healing occurs. I wish, oh I wish, that such a group had existed for me way back then, for if so I might not have ended up with what is now called post traumatic stress disorder – with the chronic depression and all that usually goes with it.

A group focused on the loss of a child might have provided me an opportunity to find solace and peace, not only through the sharing of my own struggles, but through listening to the struggles of others striving to move through it to get beyond it, with the ultimate goal that we might use, like in judo, the moves of the Evil One against him.

In effect, this is one reason we've created this resource for you. Not only do we wish to encourage you on your own journey by sharing our stories (in this case in print), but we really hope that you will take seriously the opportunity for ministry to others who are hurting, by providing opportunities where they can share, and be cared for, and find peace and hope, and a reason to carry that peace and hope to others. We hope that this book, with its stories, reflection questions, and resources in the appendix will help you to help others, because that is what Jesus would do.

We love that description of His approach to those who are broken and feel like their lives are about to be snuffed out: "A bruised reed he will not break, and a smoldering wick he will not snuff out (Matt. 12:20, NIV). That is what ministry to others in His name is about – mending the bruised reed, relighting the dying flame of faith. You can be His ally in this process by establishing a context in which people are safe to share their stories, and you are safe to do so, too.

Questions for personal reflection and/or discussion:

1. If you have ever felt like a bruised reed or a smoldering wick, share that experience with others in your group.

2. If you have sometimes felt bruised or broken, who did you feel best understood you?

3. If you could ask anything of the Lord in relation to where you are today, what would it be? Write this on a 3x5 card, anonymously.

4. If you believe that God causes all things to work together for good for those who love Him, what good things have come out of your experience of loss thus far? Share these things with your group.

5. Redistribute the 3x5 cards randomly, read them aloud one by one, and then pray for the needs that have been expressed as a way of closing your final session. Keep the card that you receive in a safe place, and pray for that need as the Lord brings it to your mind.

HOW TO USE THIS BOOK
Creating a "Tell Your Story" Forum in Your Community

This chapter describes the many places and settings where personal story sharing can be instituted and its value highlighted in the particular situation. Since it is done intentionally, the role of a facilitator is outlined with recommendations for optimum prompting of story sharing.

Forums by which people gather for the sole purpose of telling their stories abound. The extent of their benefits depend very much on the creativity and motivation of one or two people in making such an opportunity for sharing. It is with "tongue in cheek" that I say "sole purpose," since it is quite clear that when people gather to tell their stories, many purposes are fulfilled. These include establishment relationships, promoting mutual consolation, developing a sense of universality among members, information sharing, catharsis through talking, and reconstructing one's own narrative from a healthier perspective.

Nonetheless, a forum should look like a group gathered to share personal stories without any promise for anyone to make connections or interpretations. This goal may be hampered by the very process of gathering people together to share their stories. Therefore, storytelling is sometimes more natural in already established meetings. These situations are already built on common interests, motivation for attendance, or at least a "captive audience."

Churches offer many possible settings for storytelling. They are places where the "personal testimony" is understood as a person's biography focused on his or her faith journey, conversion experience, or other unique events that have reshaped their spiritual lives. These stories have genuine appeal to others either because they reinforce the faith everyone in the group holds, share scriptural wisdom that has universal application, or captivate others with unusual experiences or struggles.

A forum motif can be easily inserted, on occasion, in worship services, in established cell groups, youth events, or specialized ministries or programs. Women's groups are often fertile ground for such forums. Luncheons, Bible studies, focused group meetings, retreats, and conferences create settings conducive to telling one's story. The stories often are in response to topics taught or introduced by a speaker, and may be akin to debriefing sessions.

Academic settings ranging from a pre-kindergarten class to the university campus and seminary are important established venues for a "Tell Your Story" forum. In fact, an academic setting devoted solely to the imparting of information, without attention to the richness of student life narratives, cannot properly prepare students for career or professional goals even in highly technical or scientific education. Doctors who train in the biological sciences without attention to human issues are ill-prepared to meet even the basic medical needs of their patients. Engineers and architects cannot understand the spatial and aesthetic needs of those who will dwell in their created structures without having a basic understanding of human needs. This social education can complement the rigors of design and can be accomplished in "Telling Your Story" forums. Of particular import is the story forum in helping communities design space for the special needs of the physically and emotionally challenged. The subjects being served are the best educators of those who design.

Families are often the center of "storytelling," whether it be at the nightly dinner table or in large family gatherings for holidays and celebrations. If done well, these gatherings are places where stories originate and are passed from one person to another as news updates, and also as legacies from one generation to another. Story telling and listening promote the bonds that bring family members together. They provide validation and comfort, and help to normalize relationships when conflicts occur. Family members expect to share information, discuss pressing problems, or simply to recap shared memories. These events are often the most treasured memories that family members remember through the years. For example, who can forget Grandpa's storytelling to the family gathered around a campfire on a warm summer evening, with the marshmallows and hot dogs and watermelon and all the rest?

Developing a "Tell Your Story" Forum in an Established Setting

What are the elements helpful to setting up a forum in an established venue? The major advantage in such venues is that one does not need to create a new group setting There is already a captive audience. In this setting, the first requirement is that someone must be motivated to initiate storytelling. This person creates an environment where listening in a non-judgmental way is encouraged on the part of those not telling the story, asking only occasional questions to encourage elaboration by the teller. There should be no effort made to stop the process once begun. If the process must stop due to lack of time, then opportunities should be created for the storyteller to continue at a later time.

The second requirement is that the participants should have some common interest. The connection can be tight or loose, and the possible connections are wide ranging. Some examples include kinship, age, profession, national origin, gender, and common problems. Commonality is not crucial to successful "Tell Your Story" forums if the facilitator is adept at creating interest in a common purpose for the group, even if it is as simple as learning to tell or listen to stories. Rationales I have used include getting to know each other, learning communication skills, learning how to present one's story in another language, solidifying bonds for a mutual purpose, having effective prayer sessions, and/or meeting therapeutic goals. Once the participants accept the stated goal and have a reasonable sense of comfort in sharing, the process will begin without much effort. In fact, the forum takes advantage of the fact that many people have stories of their lives to tell and yearn for a place to tell them.

Conferences are great venues for telling your story forums. The plethora of conferences convening to address job training, professional or guild matters, political, religious, trade, research, government, or educational issues bring together a large number of people – some known to each other, some complete strangers. In these settings, the "Tell Your Story" forum can bridge the gap and sense of isolation that can often take place in large conventions. It is quite possible that people often create informal settings to connect with each other over meals and in hotel lobbies. Intentional facilitation of such forums can be an asset to atmosphere, networking, and even productivity of the conference. Well-planned facilitation that takes into account time schedules, conducive environments, purposeful motivation, and other incentives can bring the "Tell Your Story" forum to life. Once a person begins his or her narrative, others often follow suit because a level of acceptance of the idea, comfort, and even trust develops.

The role of a facilitator is to motivate the group in telling their narratives. The following are points for such a person to implement:

1. Convey clearly the reasons for the forum. The facilitator introduces the purpose of the forum in order to give the group a starting point and some direction. This can be done in a few short statements which can address any of the following: a) The facilitator may choose to highlight the goal of the organization for which narrative telling will be useful to the tasks at hand; b) The facilitator may indicate that telling one's story will enhance relationships in the group. In other words, the stated reason for the forum may simply be that the group is gathered together just to share their stories in order to get to know each other. The facilitator must be careful not to prolong this introduction to permit time for the actual narrative telling from each individual.

2. Provide a sense of the commonality. This is particularly important when people who do not know each other are gathered together for a forum. The facilitator tries to remove initial discomfort, hesitancy about self-revelation, or any awkwardness by highlighting issues, traits, or purposes that the members have in common. In some diverse groups, commonalities may not be so apparent in the beginning, but these commonalities may be revealed as the process evolves, and the facilitator can point them out along the way. Obvious commonalities pertaining to the established venues for the forum are easy to point out.

3. Address telling and listening as tasks important to each other. Since everybody has a personal story of their life, no one is un-

equipped to participate. By issuing the task of simply telling one's story, the facilitator impresses on the group that their contribution of their story is the task and very do-able. Not only so, but the other participants actually *want* to heart their story.

4. Be sensitive to the shyness level of each member, and encourage or discourage speaking versus listening. Here is where the facilitator needs to have an intuitive sense of the participants' adeptness in speaking comfortably if he does not know his audience. Usually the most vocal or socially skilled person has no problems if asked to share his story first. One should not choose the shyest person in the audience, though one does not automatically have to pick the most vocal. Perhaps someone in the average range of comfort would be most suitable. If it isn't clear who should go first, the facilitator can ask for volunteers and choose one. There is also the possibility that the facilitator may elect to be the first as a model for others.

5. Have a good sense of timing as to when questions can be asked, e.g. not too early. One wants to offer the presenter ample amount of time to tell his or her narrative. Interrupting too early, unless it is for clarification, may disturb the flow of the narrative. The facilitator must show the group how to listen by being silent for long periods of time while the presenter is speaking. There should be no hesitation to ask others to hold their questions until the end.

6. Be appreciative and encourage others to be appreciative of the teller's efforts to share.

7. Reiterate what the teller is saying if there seems to be any confusion regarding the story. Reiteration is a good way to clarify confusion, while at the same time giving the speaker a sense that he is being heard. The facilitator can do this, or the facilitator may ask another group member if they were able to understand what the speaker has just said. Then the speaker will have the opportunity to further enlighten the listeners regarding the narrative.

8. During the question and answer time at the end of each story, ask others if they understand what is being said in order to facilitate questions that clarify and amplify the narrative. The facilita-

tor can also prepare or ask some reflection questions for the group to discuss.

9. Model a non-judgmental stance, The facilitator must do this in order to keep the audience from reacting to the speaker's story, especially when there is a disagreement in lifestyle, personal philosophy, or point of view. The group needs to understand that "Tell Your Story" forums are not arenas for debate, but rather opportunities for sharing and listening to personal narratives.

10. Have attractive appearance or wear the appropriate attire common to the participants. Be a leader/facilitator without looking like one

11. If your story is not being shared at this meeting, make efforts to minimize your story and accentuate someone else's telling of their narrative. (This does not apply if you choose to use your own story to begin the forum.)

12. Discourage excessive interruption in a gentle way, always promoting the agenda of hearing the story as it unfolds in the teller's narrative.

13. Allow for prayer if appropriate to begin or end the session, inviting God to give success, benefit, and wisdom in the forum.

14. Assess the desire or need to have a subsequent forum. This opportunity for continuation accentuates the importance and legitimacy of such forums and underscores the notion that the contribution of each person's narrative had value and worth, warranting other opportunities for others to tell their stories.

15. Choose appropriate timing for a forum, e.g. when participants are relatively alert and not hungry (unless meals or snacks, coffee/tea are provided).

16. Encourage participants to concentrate on telling their story rather than discussing subject matters or advice giving. This can be done to a limited extent and for the purpose of strengthening the forum for sharing narratives.

Intentional facilitation of storytelling, if done well, will provide unique opportunities for people to benefit from each other's lives and enhance the other purposes of all gatherings. Next we look at how to start a brand new "Tell Your Story" forum in your community.

Organizing a Brand New "Tell Your Story" Forum

Giving people a chance to tell their stories strengthens existing bonds, develops new friendships, enhances fellowship, and networking, and promotes personal growth. Organizing a forum in which this takes place requires preparation, forethought, advertising, and legwork . . . but the rewards are significant. A single event may stand alone, or it may be the starting point for a new idea, project, or ministry.

What is involved in the preparation? An easy way to start is to organize the event around a guest speaker with an interesting and relevant life story to tell. Promotion of this event should begin early enough to assess the types of participants expected and some idea of the numbers, although the latter can be wide ranging from very few as in a small group to a very large number. The event planners must decide whom to invite as a target audience. They could be a homogeneous group with direct connections to the speaker, or a group amassed because they are the same gender, or a group of the same age range. They could be simply friends that the planners group wants to reach.

The first part of the event may be simply having the audience listen to the speaker tell his or her narrative. During this time, the audience will have personal reactions to the speaker's story that connect in some way with their own personal stories. Usually, there is a desire to ask questions of the speaker, but often it is because the questioning allows them to tell their story of struggle or success. These natural desires are served quite well not only in a Q&A session, but also by dividing the audience into small groups of four to eight persons with the assignment of telling each other their stories. This leads to sharing, discovering, and interacting, which benefit many of the participants in different ways. Some can experience comfort, while others receive advice. Some learn new coping strategies, or learn information or scriptural applications they had never considered. Some may benefit by making new friends with shared common interests. Of course, in a church or ministry setting some will be exposed to the Christian faith for the first time, as these "Tell Your Story" forums" can be open to all. Everyone has a story to tell. No one is unequipped.

The location for such a forum is important. It needs to be comfortable, easy to get to, and conducive for people to have nourishment, either in a coffee/tea break or as a light meal, if possible. It should be a place large enough to accommodate the participants in a lecture format and then allow the people to break into small groups, with each group retreating to a quiet area where they can begin their sharing. The groups should not be so close together that hearing is difficult.

Do the groups need facilitators? When a forum is implemented for the first time, a facilitator should be assigned to each small group. The facilitator has some understanding of the purpose of the small groups and can move things along. Oftentimes, the facilitator can be part of the planning committee, but this is not mandatory.

A women's ministry and its development can be initiated using the "Tell Your Story" format. The connectedness created at the end of such workshops often leads women to linger around each other, hoping to have the process continue. If the planners are hoping to establish follow-up meetings, they can be announced at this time. Such follow-ups can be more goal oriented, such as women's Bible studies or women's prayer groups. They may be more general, such as women's fellowship meetings, dinners, get-togethers, or other "Tell Your Story" forums. The decision as to which follow-up to use depends largely on the needs and comfort level of the participants in the forum, and what interests are expressed.

Given the general issues described, it is important to stress that the planning of each forum should be individualized to the needs and goals of the target audience, as well as to the resources and skills of the planners. Time constraints and logistics are factors to consider. Obtaining the appropriate guest speaker to jump-start the forum is important. But an essential component is the unity and motivation among the planners to create a "Tell Your Story" forum and reap its benefits.

A graduate student decided to cull a group of women from her school in order to discuss " A Woman's Worth." She began introducing the idea to her peers and generated enthusiasm from the other women as she proposed that they would get together and discuss this subject by telling their own stories. She sent out invitations and set up a time and date for this forum. She prepared by using the Internet to find interesting materials pertaining to the subject. She collected verses from the Bible that the women would find useful. Rather than looking for a guest speaker, she elected to use her own story as a catalyst for the forum.

On the day of the event, all of the invitees who agreed to come appeared. There were snacks and drinks prepared in advance. The participants sat in a circle in a quiet room in the school. The participants seemed to share their stories easily, even though some of the struggles shared touched quite painful subjects. The women already knew each other, and a certain level of trust was already present. Mutual sharing, consolation, advice giving, and relationships developed naturally, and they all wanted to have another forum because of the successful outcome.

The student's organization of her second forum was not quite as easy. Using the same strategies, she approached a number of Hispanic women in her community and talked about having a forum intended to give women "a voice" in light of the cultural silence experienced by many of them who had been in abuse situations. There was a lot of verbal interest and excitement about the forum. Many indicated that the topic was very relevant. Invitations were given to attend a dinner in the student's home. On the day of the event, only half of the invitees showed up, and all except one were late by at least two hours. Perhaps these difficulties were due to the subject matter proposed. Perhaps the cultural mindset of the invitees played a role. Perhaps the fact that these women were used to not having "a voice" meant that even when there was an opportunity to have a voice, they deprived themselves of the chance. The personalities of the participants, topic, or other factors may affect the outcome of the forum. The organizer reflected that if it had been simply an invitation to a dinner party or a birthday celebration, almost all of the invitees would have come. In retrospect, not all opportunities for narrative exchange need to have a topic focus. Sometimes an informal get-together may prove to be the best venue for successful exchanges. Using that approach, there are fewer barriers to cause doubt about attending.

As it turns out, the "voice" forum proceeded despite the lateness of the six women. It went very well with open mutual sharing. Each woman shared her story of overcoming her past abuse. They all felt that more of these opportunities should occur. The student was surprised and somewhat dubious about doing this again, given the unexpected problems, but these trials are good learning experiences for the future organization of other "Tell Your Story" forums.

May this book empower readers to create inspirational, faith-strengthening narrative opportunities to glorify Christ.

ABOUT THE AUTHORS:

Elaine Leong Eng, MD, is a Distinguished Fellow of the American Psychiatric Association. She is a graduate of Princeton University and the Albert Einstein College of Medicine. She is currently Clinical Assistant Professor of Psychiatry in the Department of Obstetrics and Gynecology at Weill-Cornell Medical College and teaches at the Alliance Theological Seminary's Graduate School of Counseling. Trained in the Lay Ministry Program of Concordia College, Dr. Eng integrates faith, medical, and psychological issues to provide mental health education to many audiences. Avenues for this include international and domestic travel for speaking engagements and writing. Her book *"Martha, Martha": How Christians Worry* is a text on anxiety disorders and the church community. Her second book is entitled *A Christian Approach to Overcoming Disability: A Doctor's Story*.

David B. Biebel, DMin, is a minister, medical editor, health educator, and author or coauthor of seventeen other books including the CBA Gold Medallion award winning *New Light on Depression* and several others that have received special recognition including *If God Is So Good, Why Do I Hurt So Bad?* and *Simple Health*. His first published book was *Jonathan, You Left Too Soon*, upon which much of his chapter in this book is based. He holds a Doctor of Ministry degree, with distinction (1986) in Personal Wholeness from Gordon-Conwell Theological Seminary. In 2008, he founded Healthy Life Press (www.healthylifepress.com) with the goal of publishing and promoting resources that can contribute to optimal health – physically, emotionally, relationally, and spiritually. New authors are welcome.

ABOUT THE CONTRIBUTORS:

Dee Brestin is a bestselling author and speaker. Her latest book, *The God of All Comfort: Finding your Way into His Arms* (Zondervan) shares her grief journey after her husband's death, and how the psalms of lament took her through the storm. Steve Brestin was a leading orthopedic surgeon in Nebraska who practiced with three other Christian orthopedists. Author Carol Kent wrote: "This book will be an instant classic for those who are hurting." Other books she has written include: *The Friendships of Women* and *A Woman of Worship* (study on the Psalms). You can learn about her ministry by visiting: (www.deebrestin.com/).

Lisa Copen is the founder of Rest Ministries, a non-profit ministry that encourages people with chronic illness. The organization's website is: (www.restministries.com/). Lisa has authored eight books, the proceeds from which support the ministry. Her books and other resources are available at: (http://chronicillnessbooks.com/.)

Lynn Eib is a journalist, cancer patient advocate, cancer- and grief-support group facilitator, and longtime colon cancer survivor. She is the author of *When God & Cancer Meet: True stories of hope and healing; Finding the Light in Cancer's Shadow: Hope, humor and healing after treatment;* and *When God & Grief Meet: True stories of comfort & courage.* She also wrote the inspirational commentary for *He Cares,* a specialized version of the New Testament, Psalms, and Proverbs for people dealing with serious/chronic illness. She has spoken throughout the country on the subject of faith and medicine and presents half-day seminars for cancer patients or grievers and those who minister to them.

Her website (http://CancerPatientAdvocate.com) is dedicated to helping people provide emotional and spiritual encouragement to patients and their caregivers, especially those facing cancer. It includes information about patient advocacy, as well as resources for those wishing to start, facilitate, or find a faith-based cancer support group.

Sue Foster, MA, LMFT, holds a Master's Degree in Marriage and Family Therapy from Alliant International University in San Diego, California, and is a licensed therapist in Tennessee and California. She co-authored *Finding Your Way After the Suicide of Someone You Love*, having lost her nineteen-year-old daughter, Shannon, to suicide in 1991. Sue has a private therapy practice and also works part-time for Music for the Soul as office manager and on-site therapist. Sue volunteers with the Tennessee Suicide Prevention Network, leads faith-based suicide support groups and grief workshops, and speaks on suicide and grieving at conferences and community forums.

Linda S. Gill, RN, MSN, MA, LPC, is a nurse, educator, licensed professional counselor, speaker, and author of the book *Mommy, What's 'Died'? The Butterfly Story*. She holds master's degrees in parent-infant nursing (1987) from the University of North Carolina at Greensboro and in clinical counseling (2003) from Columbia International University, Columbia, SC. Since 1987 she has specialized in helping individuals and families who have experienced crisis, grief, and loss, first as a hospital-based clinical nurse specialist, and now as a licensed professional counselor. In 2002, she founded the non-profit organization "Joy in the Mourning"® Center for Life Losses with the goal of helping people return to the joy of living after having experienced life-changing losses. See: (www.joyinthemourningcenter.org).

Margaret H. (Peggy) Hartshorn, PhD, became involved in the pro-life movement when she heard Roe v. Wade announced on the radio, January 22, 1973. Peggy and her husband Mike began housing pregnant women in their home and then established a pregnancy resource center in Columbus, Ohio. In 1993, after twenty years as a college English and Humanities professor, Peggy left her career to lead Heartbeat International, the first life-affirming pregnancy help network founded in the USA and the most expansive in the world with over 1,100 affiliates in forty-six countries. It is a Christ-centered association of pregnancy help centers, medical clinics, maternity homes, nonprofit adoption agencies, and abortion recovery programs. See: (www.heartbeatinternational.org).

Ronda Knuth told the story of her first husband in *The Unmasking: Married to a Rapist* by Kevin Flynn. Ronda is founder of "The Billy Blanket Project," a grassroots ministry in memory of her two babies and named after her stillborn son whom she would have called Billy. Ronda has spoken at numerous women's retreats, luncheons, etc., and is a frequent speaker for MOPS (Mothers of Preschoolers) groups in the Rocky Mountain region. Ronda has appeared on numerous radio and television programs, including "The 700 Club," "Sally Jesse Raphael," "Phil Donahue," and "Inside Edition." She lives in Denver, Colorado, with her husband, Rob. She is mother to four, grandmother to two. To contact Ronda, e-mail: blankets4healing@hotmail.com.

Alison La Frence, MD, is a volunteer Family Physician. She currently is working as the Interim Executive Director of the Alpha Crisis Pregnancy Center and Maternity Home, Savage, Minnesota. She and her husband, John Edwards, MD, travel to Cameroon, Africa for four to six weeks a year as medical missionaries.

ORGANIZATIONS

The Christian Medical and Dental Associations (CMDA) is a national organization of over 17,000 Christian physicians, dentists, healthcare professionals, and students whose purpose is to change hearts in healthcare. Founded in 1931 by two Northwestern medical students, CMDA now has over forty different outreaches. The core ministry is working with students in over 241 medical and dental school campuses across the country in an effort to create the kind of doctors we all want – physicians and dentists who are competent, compassionate, and focus on the patient more than the disease. CMDA trains students and graduates in leadership skills for effective practice and ministry. CMDA provides annual regional conferences to train student leaders to lead their campus ministries. Each year CMDA organizes and leads fifty international medical-dental teams, helps start clinics for the underserved, and sponsors students and resident rotations in developing countries. Over 500 of its members are career missionary doctors. Educating our members is an important part of our mission. CMDA produces and distributes educational and inspirational resources; provides missionary doctors with continuing education resources; and, conducts international academic exchange programs. CMDA serves as the voice of its members to the media, churches, and government – speaking out on bioethical and human rights issues. It does over 400 TV, radio, and print interviews each year and provides experts for congressional testimony. For more information go to: (www.cmda.org).

Focus on the Family is a non-profit Christian organization with a vision for healing brokenness in families, communities, and societies worldwide through Christ. The purpose of the ministry is to strengthen, defend, and celebrate the institution of the family and to highlight the unique and irreplaceable role that it plays in God's larger story of the gospel of Jesus Christ. Focus places special emphasis on marriage and parenthood, endeavoring to inspire and equip married couples to live out God's design and intention for biblical marriage and to help parents raise children who know, love, and serve God.

Through radio broadcasts, websites, conferences, magazines, and books, many have shared their personal stories of challenge and overcoming in these matters. Focus on the Family's counseling department assists many who call with their stories of struggle. Trained, supportive staff give the callers their loving attention and can refer people to sources of help in their location.

To speak with a counselor, please call (800) A-FAMILY (232-6459) between 6:00 AM and 8:00 PM Mountain Time, and ask for a counselor's assistant. Don't be discouraged if she requests that you allow a counselor to call you back. One of them will contact you just as soon as possible. Both this service and the return call are offered at no cost to you.

You can write to Focus on the Family at 8605 Explorer Drive, Colorado Springs, CO, 80920. You can also learn more about the ministry of Focus on the Family by visiting (www.focusonthefamily.com).

Heartbeat International advances the pregnancy help movement worldwide. Heartbeat provides leadership training; resources; special help for international pregnancy help centers and centers in urban neighborhoods; defense and representation of pregnancy centers; and Option Line (1-800-395-HELP, 1-800-395-4357), a 24/7 hotline to connect those in need with their local pregnancy help centers. See (www.heartbeatinternational.org) and (www.optionline.org) or call 1-888-885-7577 for more information.

Resources from Healthy Life Press

We've Got Mail: The New Testament Letters in
Modern English - As Relevant Today as Ever!
by Rev. Warren C. Biebel Jr. (Printed: $9.95;
PDF eBook: $6.95; together: $15.00 at
www.healthylifepress.com). *We've Got Mail* is a new para-
phrase of the New Testament Letters, in modern English, especially
designed to inspire in readers a loving appreciation for God's Word.

Hearth & Home - Recipes for Life - by Karey Swan
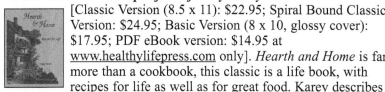
[Classic Version (8.5 x 11): $22.95; Spiral Bound Classic
Version: $24.95; Basic Version (8 x 10, glossy cover):
$17.95; PDF eBook version: $14.95 at
www.healthylifepress.com only]. *Hearth and Home* is far
more than a cookbook, this classic is a life book, with
recipes for life as well as for great food. Karey describes
how to buy and prepare from scratch a wide variety of tantalizing dishes, while weaving into the book's fabric the wisdom of the ages plus the
recipe that she and her husband, Monte (author of *Romancing Your
Child's Heart*) used to raise their kids. A great gift for Christmas or for a
new bride.

Who Me, Pray? Prayer 101:
Praying Aloud, for Beginners -
by Gary A. Burlingame (Printed: $6.95 eBook:
$2.99 - together $7.95 at www.healthylifepress.com). *Who
Me, Pray?* is a practical guide for prayer, based on Jesus'
direction in "The Lord's Prayer," with examples provided for
use in typical situations where you might be asked or expected to pray
in public.

The Big Black Book - What the Christmas Tree Saw -

by Rev. Warren C. Biebel Jr (Printed: $7.95; PDF eBook:
$4.95; Together: $10.95 at www.healthylifepress.com). An
original Christmas story, from the perspective of the
Christmas tree. This little book is especially suitable for parents to read to their children on Christmas eve or Christmas
day, though the message of the book is appropriate year-
round.

My Broken Heart Sings, the poetry of Gary Burlingame (Printed: $10.95; PDF eBook: $6.95; Together: $13.95 at www.healthylifepress.com). In 1987, Gary and his wife Debbie lost their son Christopher John, at only six months of age, to a chronic lung disease. This life-changing experience gave them a special heart for helping others through similar loss and pain. Some of Gary's poems speak directly out of their own sorrow while other poems speak for those who were unable to give voice to their pain.

After Normal: One Teen's Journey Following Her Brother's Death - by Diane Aggen (Printed: $11.95; eBook:$5.95; together: $15.00 at www.healthylifepress.com). *After Normal* is based on a journal the author kept following the death of her brother. It offers helpful insights and understanding for teens facing a similar loss or for those who might wish to understand and help teens facing a similar loss.

In the Unlikely Event of a Water Landing - Lessons Learned from Landing in the Hudson River - by Andrew Jamison, MD (Printed: $8.95; PDF eBook: $6.95; Together: $12.95 at www.healthylifepress.com). Dr. Andrew Jamison was flying standby on US Airways Flight 1549 toward Charlotte on January 15, 2009, from New York City, where he had been interviewing for a residency position. Little did he know that the next stop would be the Hudson River. This is one person's account of first-hand lessons learned about the sovereignty of God over all things. Riveting and inspirational, this book would be especially helpful for people facing adversity, and in need of hope and encouragement.

Finding Martians in the Dark — Everything I Needed to Know About Teaching Took Me Only 30 Years to Learn - by Dan M. Biebel (Printed: $10.95; PDF eBook: $6.95; Together: $15.00 at www.healthylifepress.com). Available March 2010. Packed with wise advice based on hard experience, and laced with humor, this book, suited for new and used teachers, is destined to become an instant classic and required reading at teacher training institutions. Susan J. Wegmann, Ph.D. says, "Biebel's sardonic wit is mellowed by a genuine love for kids and teaching... A Whitman-like sensibility flows through his stories of teaching, learning, and life."

6274867R0

Made in the USA
Charleston, SC
05 October 2010